THE WHOLE DUDE

THE WHOLE DUDE

David Ketcherside

Awake New Media

Copyright © 2022 by David Ketcherside.

All rights reserved, including the right of reproduction in whole or in part in any form. No part of this book may be reproduced in any form without written permission of the publisher.

ISBN: 979-8-218-00200-8 (paperback)

Cover Illustration by Michael Behrens
Copyright © 2022 by Awake New Media

Manufactured in the United States of America

Publisher
Awake New Media

www.thewholedude.com

Contents

Introduction vii
PART ONE - The Son 11
  Introducing the Son Wake Rider 13
  The Son's Desire 14
  Who Comes to Mind When I Think of the Son Wake Rider 15
  Why This is Important 16
  The Son's Core Strength 17
  Our Soundtrack 18
Chapter One—A Return to Innocence 19
  Son Ideal Number One—Purity 19
  Son Distortion Number One—Dirty 21
    What I Did Before 21
    What I Do Now 23
    What I Did Before 23
    What I Do Now 24
  Son Distortion Number Two—Naive 25
    What I Did Before 26
    What I Do Now 27
  Rider Reminders 27
Chapter Two—Ask the Next Question 28
  Son Ideal Number Two - Wonderment 28
  Son Distortion Number Three—Believing You Are Dumb 29
    What I Did Before 30
    What I Do Now 31
  Son Distortion Number Four—Being a Know it All 32
    What I Did Before 33
    What I Do Now 34
  Rider Reminders 34
Chapter Three—From the Mouths of Babes 35
  Son Ideal Number Three—Honesty 35
    What I Did Before 35
    What I Do Now 36
  Son Distortion Number Five—Lies to Self 37
    What I Did Before 37

What I Do Now	38
Son Distortion Number Six—Lies to Others	39
Rider Reminders	40
Chapter Four—Boys... Just Wanna Have Fun	41
Son Ideal Number Four—Fun	41
Son Distortion Number Seven—Dull	43
What I Did Before	44
What I Do Now	45
Son Distortion Number Eight—Reckless	45
What I Did Before	45
What I Do Now	47
Rider Reminders	48
Son Section Takeaways	49
The First B Word—Beliefs	49
Rite of Passage	51
Exercise	52
PART TWO - The Warrior	53
The Warrior's Journey	55
The Warrior's Desire	56
Why This Is Important	56
Who Comes to Mind When I Think of the Warrior Wake Rider	57
The Warrior's Core Strength	58
Gonna Fly Now	58
Chapter Five—Managing Monsters	61
Warrior Ideal Number One—Courage	61
Warrior Distortion Number One—Fearful	64
What I Did Before	65
What I Do Now	66
What I Did Before	67
What I Do Now	67
What I Did Before	68
What I Do Now	68
Warrior Distortion Number Two—Being Overly Aggressive	69
What I Did Before	69
What I Do Now	70
Rider Reminders	72
Chapter Six—Rome Wasn't Built in a Day	73
Warrior Ideal Number Two—Integrity	73
Warrior Distortion Number Three—Low Standards	79

What I Did Before 81
What I Do Now 81
Warrior Distortion Number Four—Arrogance 82
Rider Reminders 84
Chapter Seven—Your Strength is in the Pause 85
Warrior Ideal Number Three—Grace Under Pressure.............85
What I Did Before: 89
What I Do Now:..89
Warrior Distortion Number Six—Agitated...............................90
What I Did Before: 91
What I Do Now:..92
What I Did Before: 93
What I Do Now 93
Rider Reminders 95
Chapter Eight—Conflict is a Part of Life 96
Warrior Ideal Number Four—Diplomat 96
Warrior Distortion Number Seven—Avoids Conflict................98
What I Used to Do 101
What I Do Now 102
Warrior Distortion Number Eight—Won't Budge 103
Rider Reminders 105
Warrior Section Takeaways 106
The Second B Word—Bearings..106
Rite of Passage..108
Exercise 108
PART THREE - The Lover 109
The Lover's Transformation 111
The Lover's Desire 112
Why This Is Important 114
Who comes to mind when I think of the Lover Wake Rider 116
Core Strength of the Lover..117
The Sweetness of Life 118
Chapter Nine—I'm Speechless..121
Lover Ideal Number One—Patience 121
Lover Distortion Number One—Doesn't Express 123
What I Did Before 124
What I Do Now 124
Lover Distortion Number Two—Control Issues 125
What I Did Before 126

iii

    What I Do Now 128
    Rider Reminders 128
  Chapter Ten—What No One Taught Us 129
    Lover Ideal Number Two—Self-Love 129
      What I Used To Do 131
      What I Do Now 131
    Lover Distortion Number Three—Unworthy 133
      What I Did Before 134
      What I Do Now 135
    Lover Distortion Number Four—Outside Validation 137
      What I Did Before 137
      What I Do Now 138
      What I Did Before 139
      What I Do Now 140
    Rider Reminders 143
  Chapter Eleven—Addition Through Subtraction 144
    Lover Ideal Number Three—Unattached 144
      What I Did Before 146
      What I Do Now 147
    Lover Distortion Number Five—Fear of Loss 148
      What I Did Before 148
      What I Do Now 149
    Lover Distortion Number Six—Obsession 150
      What I Did Before 151
      What I Do Now 151
    Rider Reminders 152
  Chapter Twelve—SEX... Yes Please 153
    Lover Ideal Number Four—Sacred 153
    Lover Distortion Number Seven—Putting up walls 163
      What I Did Before 164
      What I Do Now 165
    Lover Distortion Number Eight—Unfaithful 165
    Rider Reminders 167
Lover Section Takeaways 168
  The Third B Word—Being 168
  Rite of Passage 169
  Exercise 169
PART FOUR - The Father 171
The Father Wake Rider 173

Introducing the Father 173
The Father's Desire.. 174
Why This is Important.. 176
Who Comes to Mind When I Think of the Father Wake Rider 178
Core Strength of the Father 178
Amazon Therapy 179
Chapter Thirteen—I'm Done Hurting Myself 186
    What I Used to Do 187
    What I Do Now 189
    Father Distortion Number One—Too Hurt............................ 191
    Father Distortion Number Two—Vengeful........................... 194
    Rider Reminders 196
Chapter Fourteen—Look Beyond Religion 197
    Father Ideal Number Two—Spiritual 197
    What I Used To Do.. 198
    What I Do Now 199
    Father Distortion Number Three—Too Materialistic 202
    What I Did Before 205
    What I Do Now 205
    Father Distortion Number Four—Self-Righteous 206
    What I Did Before 209
    What I Do Now 209
    Rider Reminders 210
Chapter Fifteen—The Only Thing a Father Owes His Children.211
    Father Ideal Number Three—Legacy-Minded...................... 211
    What I Did Before 212
    What I Do Now 213
    What I Did Before 214
    What I Do Now 215
    Father Distortion Number Five—Apathy 216
    Father Distortion Number Six—Skepticism 218
    What I Did Before 219
    What I Do Now 219
    Rider Reminders 221
Chapter Sixteen—My New Superpower.................................... 222
    Father Ideal Number Four—Infinite 222
    Father Distortion Number Seven—Scarcity Mentality 226
    Father Distortion Number Eight—Idol Worship 228
    What I Did Before 230

v

    What I Do Now 231
    Rider Reminders 232
Father Section Takeaways 233
    The Fourth B Word—Beyond 233
    Rite of Passage 233
    Exercise 234
EXTRAS 239
Verification 241
Understanding Energy 243
Acknowledgements 247
Book Suggestions 249
References 251

Introduction

"Please allow me to introduce myself, I'm a man of wealth and taste." —Mick Jagger [1]

Maybe if I'm lucky someday I'll have a lot of material wealth like Jagger, but in the meantime I'm grateful for the ride I've been on and all the non-material wealth I've acquired along the way. What I mean by that is, I've had the good fortune to live a pretty exquisite, yet unconventional life. This is important because it seems like we are now living in a world where *unconventional* is becoming the norm. We are all asking: "Is there more to this life? Is this all there is? What's next? Will I ever *arrive*?"

The most daunting part of this new era is that it is overwhelming due to all of the information available and all the options that we have. It seems like everything is evolving and in constant motion and as a result, it's hard to grasp the concept of what feeling whole is. We feel fragmented because there is an endless stream of decisions we need to make. "Should I buy a house or rent? Should I go back to school? Should I get a Diet Pepsi or Coke Zero? Should I tell my boss he's an idiot or just keep my mouth shut and let another piece of my soul die?"

We have access to answers to every question right at our fingertips, but we fear we'll make the wrong decision. We don't know if something is the *truth* or an *alternative fact*.

We have trust issues.

Trust is at a premium. We are surrounded by a lot of so-called experts and unknown variables, and it is hard to take a leap of faith to form and usher in new beliefs that can help us in this new way of being.

I feel this is where the majority of the world is emotionally right now. In my opinion, the biggest advantage we can give ourselves is to be completely okay and comfortable with the unknown. If we can get to that point, we can begin to trust *ourselves* and we do this by remembering who we are. The good news is that we aren't broken like society tells us, instead, I believe we are whole already. We just need reminders so we can remember what that feels like. My aim is to depict this for you in this book.

When I first started writing this book I really wanted to understand how it could be different from all of the other personal development books. There are obviously some outstanding coaches and mentors out there, but I knew there was something else I could offer people who are on a path of self discovery and personal growth.

I wanted to explain how my presence as a man changed and how I've been able to show up with more authentic confidence in a variety of situations. Whether I needed grit to finish a project on time, or to show mercy to one of my daughters for what might be deemed a screw-up. I began to really embrace my true self because I knew that all of these parts working together are what made me, *me*.

My goal for this book is to:
- Discuss very foundational concepts that are at the root of all of us
- To present a model that acts as a quick reference

To achieve these goals, I've created a relatable framework so you can recognize what being whole is. There are four sections to this and I created an avatar for each section and I call them Wake Riders. They illustrate the ideal ways that we can show up and react to any given situation. We can show up as the Son, Warrior, Lover, or Father.

The essence of each Wake Rider is:

- The *Son* is about the qualities of something brand new and fresh
- The *Warrior* is about that drive we have to achieve what we want
- The *Lover* is about enjoying and appreciating the richness of life
- The *Father* is about being able to see past our current situation and finding peace

Through storytelling I show how each is an integral part of the whole. The Wake Riders have ideal traits and we also get to see distortions of their states of being. Additionally, I discuss their desires, core strengths, rites of passages, and then share my takeaways at the end of each section.

Lastly, there is a natural progression each of the Wake Riders move through as they have experiences and grow. You can read the book from cover to cover, but I strove to write the book so each section can stand alone—by all means, if you feel so drawn, pick up at the section that relates to where you are in your life right now.

Enjoy *The Whole Dude*. I appreciate your interest in my stories.

PART ONE - The Son

The Whole Dude

The Son Wake Rider
Hitting Reset

"I'm amazed by how many individuals mess up every new day with yesterday" —*Dr. Gary Chapman.* [2]

Introducing the Son Wake Rider

The essence of the Son Wake Rider is the alive feeling we have at the beginning of something. We can tap into a completely new way of thinking anytime we choose. This could be the manner in which we face each day, or the feeling we have right after we make a major life decision. New starts might include launching a business, going back to school to learn skills, a career change, or even the decision to begin an intimate relationship.

We all have a foundational ability to hit the reset button that can give us a simple shift in perspective and this can make a huge difference in our life. This *new beginning* energy is what the Son Wake Rider is all about.

One of my goals for this section of the book is for you to start to question everything. Since you are starting this journey of being a Whole Dude, why not do a deep dive into trying to figure out how you got where you are today, and decide what you would like to be different in your life. You have the ability to create new circumstances when you realize you can change your beliefs.

The Son's Desire

When we are young we subconsciously receive a lot of information about the world that surrounds us. During this process we develop the root desire to be recognized. The Son Wake Rider is creative and wants to be seen and heard. He is learning constantly and this solidifies his identity and helps him understand his worth.

If the Son gets too attached to the desire to be seen, he develops the extreme version of this desire which is the need to be accepted.

As an adult, if our need for acceptance is unresolved, distortions can show up in a variety of ways. One way this plays out is through the *keep up with the Joneses syndrome*. This is where when the neighbor gets a new mower and you decide you must get a big built-in grill and fire pit. The other neighbor gets a new car, so you decide it is time to get a boat.

It's cool to be able to buy shiny new things, but I have to wonder if this little game is rooted in a buried need to fit in and be accepted.

Having desires isn't a bad thing and the need for recognition can be harnessed in a good way. For instance, I think it is healthy to be rewarded for a job well done. I think it is even important to acknowledge yourself for your achievements in life. The question is, how can this fundamental desire of the Son be leveraged for good and managed in a way where it doesn't turn into an unhealthy attachment?

I think a positive way to look at this desire is to leverage it and build your creativity muscles. Understand that at your very core you are an expressive being and can do beautiful and meaningful things. These talents can bring joy and satisfaction to others. Why not put your efforts into honing your skills and focusing on what you are creating, versus worrying about what other people are doing and thinking?

Desires get a bad rap and have been scorned by religious dogma as if they are immoral; yet, it is the beginning of everything. I believe that when we have a desire it is God giving us a signal to begin the process of co-creation.

I was excited to run across a quote by Betrand Russell who won a Nobel Prize in Literature for a paper he wrote about human desire. In his acceptance speech he said:

"All human activity is prompted by desire. There is a wholly fallacious theory advanced by some earnest moralists to the effect that it is possible to resist desire in the interests of duty and moral principle. I say this is fallacious, not because no man ever acts from a sense of duty, but because duty has no hold on him unless he desires to be dutiful. If you wish to know what men will do, you must know not only, or principally, their material circumstances, but rather the whole system of their desires with their relative strengths."

Desire can be a catalyst and ongoing fuel that keeps us focused on achieving great things. I believe there are positive and negative effects depending on how attached we get to a desire.

Society tells us we need to have all this physical *stuff* to feel fulfilled. We buy into this conventional way of being where we think we need to accumulate tangible things to be happy. We use our possessions as a yardstick to measure our progress. We feel like there are all these milestones we need to achieve to arrive at this magical place of completion and happiness. But we never really seem to get there.

Turn your need for recognition and acceptance inward.

Work on giving yourself attention.

Create the space you need in your life to grow and learn.

Not worrying about others' approval can help quiet your mind and help you learn with more ease.

Who Comes to Mind When I Think of the Son Wake Rider

I think all the Wake Riders have an immature and mature version. The immature version has the essence of the Wake Rider but hasn't quite embodied the lessons he's learned from the distortions. The mature Wake Rider has all four ideals in tow and is the fully developed version who is ready to transition into the next evolution of development.

An example that comes to mind for the immature Son is Mowgli from the Disney movie T*he Jungle Book*. When we think of him, we see his sense of wonder and his innocence. He encounters a variety of potential dangers on his journey but does not even realize it. The movie was so popular because Mowgli's *son-ness* is so refreshing and serves as a reminder of how we acted when we were young. We all have this potential to return to living a life of adventure and freedom. One of my favorite parts of the movie is the song "The Bare Necessities." I love how symbolic it is and serves as a reminder about how little we really need to be happy. At the root level we pretty much just need food, water, shelter, and the love of our friends and family.

An example of a Son who is a little more mature is the character named Sammy Smalls in the movie *The Sandlot*. Sammy is not as innocent as Mowgli. He is in fifth grade and just moved to a new town. He doesn't really mesh with his stepdad and he is struggling to be accepted by a group of kids who play baseball nearby. Sammy personifies the emotional turmoil, self-doubt, and the urges to fit in that young people go through. I love the movie because we learn about how baseball is such a beautiful way to connect with people. It's my favorite sport, and it's a great example of how we can share an experience with millions of other people.

Why This is Important

Our environment and the experiences we had growing up impact our identity and how we view the world. Many of us had traumas and unresolved issues from our childhood which still affect us today. Some of the ways this manifests in our adult life are worthiness issues, negative self-talk, fear of failure or rejection, and feelings of doubt. I theorize that these are related to the Son's pain points and I try to address these issues in the book. The good news is we all can adapt and grow.

Well-meaning people tell us to grow up and say "you have responsibilities" and "don't be such a baby." When we become an adult, we lose our inner Son reference points and we start taking life too seriously.

One thing I have been learning lately is how the more I feel whole, the more I see how important laughing is and how important it is to have fun! I want to incorporate more laughter into my life. I want to keep these jovial feelings no matter what age I am, even if I'm an 86-year-old man.

This crystallized for me last night when I walked into a Starbucks and younger people were working, and one kid was sitting in the drive-thru window. Literally... sitting *in* the window. I had to laugh because the grown-up in me was like "Oh my goodness, I imagine there are all kinds of OSHA violations going on here" and then the Son side of me popped up and I dropped the judgment and I cracked up. I laughed with them and I said "Oh my gosh, what a riot! That's exactly what I'd be doing!" and "It's so beautiful outside—glad you guys can have fun. I'd be hanging out the window, too."

During your first waking moments each morning, you get to decide what your day will be like. You get to choose what you are going to invite into your reality at that moment. Are you going to invite peace and calm or are you going to allow fear and anxiety to add extra pressure as you think about what you need to get done that day? By having this realization, you now know it's *you* who controls your reality!

When you are out there paddling and approaching the wakes of your new day, you can get on top of what type of emotions you let dictate your day when you *first wake up*.

The Son's Core Strength

We are all meaning makers and this starts at a very young age. We receive raw data all the time and it is the Son who determines how this information relates to yourself. You could say the Son *core relates* ideas and turns them into information. The Son learns to perceive what is good or bad, what can harm him or what is safe. (Remember Mowgli?) These experiences are what form and mold his biases, belief systems, and paints the picture he considers to be reality.

Our Soundtrack

My dad came from a generation who did not really express love very well. As a matter of fact, there were very, very, *very* few times as a kid (or throughout my life) I heard my dad say, "I love you." Therefore, as a dad myself, it's important to me to tell my kids how much I love them on a regular basis.

Childhood memories can create biases that impact how we see the world and ourselves. This includes how much we think we are worth to the world. As a child, we acquire the language and tone that we use when we talk to ourselves. This "soundtrack" then begins to play in our heads the rest of our life, and it can do a lot of good or a lot of harm.

As meaning makers we receive a stimulus and internalize the definition we gave it in our body. We are exposed to words being used by others around us and those get paired up with the images created in our head. Not only does this soundtrack interpret the meaning of words, but it also determines how we feel about ourselves. In addition to our sense of worth, our perceptions and self-talk can affect our DNA and our physiology.

In his groundbreaking book *The Biology of Belief*, Bruce Lipton writes about the experiments he conducted studying DNA, proteins, and cell membranes. Our cell membranes have receptor sites that listen for signals and they pair up proteins that go through the cell membrane and react to these signals. The cells either open themselves up and move toward healthy signals—which leads to growth—or they move away from harmful signals and close themselves up to the perceived threat—which inhibits growth. Lipton hypothesizes a signal can be a belief, and therefore, our beliefs can affect our physiology as well as our mental and emotional wellbeing.

This is why it is so important to discuss our beliefs and self-talk, which we'll get to straight away.

Chapter One—A Return to Innocence

> *"A child's world is fresh and new and beautiful, full of wonder and excitement. It is our misfortune that for most of us that clear-eyed vision, that true instinct for what is beautiful and awe-inspiring, is dimmed and even lost before we reach adulthood.." —*
> *Rachel Carson* [3]

Son Ideal Number One—Purity

I honestly think about 80–90% of all people are good. Deep down everyone probably has a pure heart. I guess the problem is we sometimes tell ourselves a story about how we are bad. We then start believing our life experiences tainted us via all the *wrongs* we've done along the way. Consequently, most of us don't realize that we can tap into a brand new blank slate that is pure, even if we feel broken or dirty.

As I was thinking about this concept this morning, I became overwhelmed when I started recording my thoughts about purity. I started getting choked up. It is hard to explain why, but I am going to try. I guess I was emotional because it was like grieving a part of me I thought didn't exist anymore like this was a former version of myself.

Then suddenly, I had this quick flash of me as an innocent child. What came to mind was a picture of my sister Lisa and me sleeping in a La-Z-Boy recliner. It was New Year's Eve and we were waiting for my Mom and Dad to come home from a party. We were kind of cuddled together there with our heads touching each other's shoulders. She with her dark hair and me with my light blond hair, just lying there sleeping. I was in my brown corduroys and my patent leather shoes. They were probably passed on from my brother Mike. We wore out our tennis shoes pretty quick back then, but the dressy leather shoes didn't get used as much, and so they lasted longer and made a good hand me down.

Then I remembered an image of me with my little towhead in a picture with my younger sister when we were really small, and I thought of how pure we were then. Shari was basically *swimming* in a bucket. I began to get teary-eyed because this reminded me of how out of touch I was with that little person. I was in my own little world back then, soaking up everything in my environment and not even aware of reality.

All there was back then was *fascination* as I was in an adventurous reality full of family picnics and church carnivals, where I spun around laughing on MoMo the Monster. A time when there was the anticipation of Christmas mornings, or waking to a quarter under my pillow left by the Tooth Fairy. And *knowing* that if I dug deep enough in the dirt in my backyard, I'd find an arrowhead, gold, fossils, or even a dinosaur bone.

I thought of all the fun I had as a kid. I remembered the picture of me by my first powder blue ten-speed bike holding my first KISS album in the foyer in our home off Lemonwood. *KISS Destroyer!* (yeah baby!). I was wearing a homemade brown cotton-polyester blend long sleeve shirt my Mom sewed for me, and all along not realizing in a few years I would be stressed about fitting in at a new school and needing to wear an Izod instead of my homemade polo style shirts. Mom did an amazing job with her sewing by the way. I just did not have the stupid alligator on my shirt that I thought was required to fit in at a West County school. To this day, at 85, my Mom is still sewing stuff and sharing her abundant love with everyone through all her sewing creations.

As I reflected on these memories, I began to understand how this young person is still a part of who I am. He still exists, and in my heart of hearts, I believe you can tap into a pure version of yourself whenever you want and can relive those feelings of youthful magic. I think all of this is still inside of us, like the original minted master copy of an album. It is there still, but society robs it from us and tells us we need to grow up.

When we buy into this conventional thinking, we stop remembering this part of ourselves and we think we aren't innocent anymore. We start to believe we are less of a man somehow if we have a childlike nature about us.

Being able to remember this early version of yourself is a very powerful tool to tap into when life gets rough. When it is all said and done, the fancy car, those new golf clubs, the boat, and the big house, all eventually lose their shine. Those things are all *stuff* and are not permanent. While they may bring us joy for a while, that feeling won't last forever. Our memories *are* permanent though because they can be shared with others and are what tie us to future generations.

Those moments of joy, love, contentment, and appreciation are all magic. When the chips are down and you're struggling, you can remember moments of purity, newness, and unadulterated joy—and when you do this, I guarantee you will smile and shift into a better mood.

Son Distortion Number One—Dirty

Most children have experiences that result in them not feeling innocent anymore such as discovering there's no Santa Claus or Easter Bunny. This could happen when a parent hurts them by yelling at them or when they find out their parents aren't perfect. Or when they catch an adult in some type of compromising activity or sexual situation deemed *dirty*.

If you label something as being dirty you tell yourself it isn't clean or pure. Think about what dirt is though. Dirt is the decomposing of material. It's the breaking down of something. This is what is going on when you feel dirty the first time. You no longer feel connected to the whole. You think you ceased to be your pure wholesome self.

What I Did Before

Speaking of breaking, my first memory of feeling *dirty* is something that had a big influence on my identity. This experience caused a lot of self-inflicted pain and was a very impactful event that occurred when I was around three and a half years old. It was the day of my little sister Shari's baptism. We lived in the city at the time and we had a detached garage. I guess I was needing attention, and me and my friend Timmy Brotherton, in our fun childlike nature, decided it would be exciting to throw rocks at all the windows in the garage.

The Whole Dude

We were mesmerized by watching the glass shatter everywhere and before long we broke out all the garage windows while all the other kids and grown-ups were having a celebration inside the house. I guess we were bored and looking for attention or whatever it was unattended boys did back in 1970. Ironically, I think I was the one who caught all the heat and Timmy did not get into trouble at all, but after this episode, I got the nickname *Dumb Stupid David*.

I was so young at the time, and this seriously affected who I thought I was. As the second youngest of seven kids, I certainly got picked on a lot by my siblings. Also, my Dad started calling me Pea-brain (and to this day I still cannot stand those stupid little *crud balls*). I do not think I got my butt whooped or physically punished, but the emotional damage was much more harmful. Buried deep on an unconscious level I felt hurt and worse, I began to accept *Dumb Stupid David* as part of who I was.

This story illustrates how experiences and environmental factors began to form the way I saw myself and the belief system I began to form in my unconscious mind. This created the *tapes* which ran in the background and dictated the tone of self-talk I had constantly in my head. All of which was formed by a misperceived belief that was reinforced by my siblings and Dad, but mostly *me*. I was no longer pure and new. I was broken.

At the very least, it had an impact on the very self-critical way I began talking to myself. For example, if I would screw something up a little voice shouted inside my head and I'd call myself *Dumb Stupid David*, and this caused me to be my harshest critic. Every time something would go wrong or if I would make a mistake, I'd yell at myself and be like "Dammit, David!" or "Come on Pea-brain, don't be so stupid." For most of my life, I have beaten myself up like this. It's no wonder I became such an *all-star* at self-deprecating humor! And...don't even get me started on the subject of people-pleasing...

What I Do Now

I realize now language creates my reality. I am more aware when I am referring to myself in a negative way and luckily catch it quicker. In a lot of cases, I just laugh now at myself when I make mistakes. I came across a quote that drives home this point recently:

"Do not speak badly of yourself, for the warrior that is inside of you hears your words and is lessened by them." — David Gemmell, Quest For Lost Heroes

What I Did Before

Another way the concept of feeling dirty affects us revolves around the shame we carry around sex. Here is a story that hardly anyone knows which is both shameful and hysterical at the same time. So...my Dad used to subscribe to *Playboy Magazine*. He was even a bonafide key holder to the Playboy Club in St. Louis in the 1970s. Membership had its privileges, as they say, and one of them was a parcel wrapped in dark blue plastic which landed in our mailbox once a month. At some point, I caught onto what was being sent to our home in that mysterious package. My Mom actually thought it was funny and wasn't threatened by any of the magazines' content or judged him as a bad person. Dad wasn't one of those guys who left that stuff laying around and he kept the magazines in this really tall and heavy dresser in his bedroom.

There was a literal trove of erotic treasures stored in his middle drawer and I developed a sneaky habit that I carried shame around for several years. I used to go through his drawer and pull out one *Playboy* at a time and get my little juvenile thrills. Thinking back on this, I don't even know when the hell I was even able to do this because we were in a house of nine people with very little privacy. But I was a stealthy little dude! I developed some serious skills at not getting caught. He kept them arranged in a random yet concise way and I would take a mental picture of exactly how they laid in the drawer. Between the tantalizing images of the beautiful women and the sheer terror I had of my Dad catching me, I'm surprised I didn't have a heart attack.

I'm pretty sure Barbi Benton was the first woman I ever saw naked. I was an especially *big* fan of the Bo Derek issue and prayed to God I could grow up to be like John Derek.

Apparently, because of all this sneakiness and social conditioning, I developed the belief that nudity was bad and I was dirty and not an innocent child anymore. And, well, yes, the nuns shaming me didn't help much either.

What I Do Now

First of all, I have tremendous respect for women, especially women who are strong and know that they are more than just their outside woman wrapper. I know women aren't property to own and show off. I also don't think of sexual relations as dirty, I now hold sex as a sacred activity between two people and don't take it lightly. A big part of the Lover section goes into relationships so you'll get a good feel there on what I do now.

A funny side note is that when my Dad passed away my Mom wanted to clear out those dresser drawers and gave me a box of my Dad's old *Playboys* and told me I might enjoy the articles. I then confessed to her the little charade I pulled off all those years as a kid and we laughed our butt off. I also like to think my Dad was looking down on me laughing too and nodding his head saying, "Yo, dude—I knew what you were doing all along."

I believe that when we lose our sense of purity we feel broken and experience hurt for the first time. We develop a need for safety and protection and I feel that is when our ego is first created. In our purest state, there is no ego. When we feel hurt for the first time, it is so alien to us and shocking, our ego gets invented and it becomes this self-anointed protector who goes out of its way to keep us safe, even if this means creating an insane litany of imaginary scenarios of ways we can potentially get hurt.

At first, we seek protection from our parents, siblings, teachers, babysitters, or even our toys. As we get a little older, we seek out the protection of being accepted by our peer group because the sense of belonging makes us feel safe.

Then as adults we want the police to protect us, and at some point, we think this is not good enough, so we get an alarm system and one of those little doorbell thingies with a camera on it. And when we start to worry that the alarm and police are not good enough, we begin feeling like we need to start buying guns in case a bad guy breaks into our house. We justify all this by telling ourselves "the police are only minutes away when seconds count."

I think avoiding being hurt and our need for protection are all byproducts of that broken feeling and it forms a belief system that plays in the background. We don't even realize how pervasive our need for safety is and how it affects many of our decisions.

The first time I read this quote by Helen Keller I was confused by it: *"Life is either a great adventure or nothing at all."*

It took several years for me to see its wisdom. I eventually interpreted it to mean that if you can, just for a moment, suspend your need for safety, you will become more present and truly live your life.

And if you don't realize this and always play it safe, you basically aren't *living.*

There is a very subtle relationship between childhood traumas and avoiding being hurt. One way we were all hurt as kids that continues to manifest in our life is the pain around not being accepted by our peers. This is a childhood wound often buried so deep we don't know it even exists. I mean, let's face it: kids can be really mean to each other. When we can heal the need to be accepted, this huge breakthrough can truly re-energize us. I talk about this more in chapter ten which is about self-love.

Son Distortion Number Two—Naive

This may sound odd, but have you ever met someone who is such a nice person they're just too nice? They tend to be gullible, and people take advantage of them (and usually they are so naive they don't even realize it). And in my opinion, this can be damaging.

If you think of Jesus Christ, he is probably one of the best examples of pureness. But he wasn't naive. The Bible talks about how Jesus favored children because of their pure and untainted nature. Also, there are parables about the lion and the lamb laying together. This seems profound how two seemingly opposite beasts could co-exist. I think it is an allegory, though trying to teach us we can embody both the tenacity and toughness of a lion and the gentleness and innocence of a lamb. Jesus was pure and holy and a great example to learn from; as he had a lot of strength, vision, and wisdom to go along with his love, compassion, and purity.

Can you see how someone can still be pure, but they don't have to be naive? Perhaps the naive person does not have enough *real world* in them to have developed the discernment they need to make proper choices. The naive person thinks ignorance is bliss and moves through life in a *gosh golly* kind of way.

I do not mean to be judging this way of being, I'm just saying it is susceptible to being taken advantage of, sadly. It is however a lovely way to be compared to being a bitter or harsh person. The price you pay for being naive can take its toll physically and emotionally though, and this could lead to getting hurt.

What I Did Before

In my early business experiences when I was younger and was brought *opportunities* and because of my naivety, I was taken advantage of—not paid enough for my work or paying too much for something because I didn't do the proper research. For example, at one point I was enrolled in a few multi-level marketing companies because I was naive, and just drank the company's Kool-Aid and bought into the dream they were selling. Before I knew it I had a closet full of products I couldn't consume fast enough or sell enough of because I was told in order to be a leader I needed to be on an auto-ship.

Another example of my naivety was my *lightworker phase.* I went through a time where I just wanted to bypass traumas and negative emotions and all I wanted to do was see what I deemed beautiful like light and love. I wanted to push this perspective out into the world and signed all my super deep emails and Facebook posts L&L- dK. And I always wanted to be this beam of light shining out into the world.

What I Do Now

My naivety changed eventually when I realized life is not just light and love. I accepted there is darkness in the world, and the true lightworker knows this and can dance in the dark during their journey. I feel like a whole dude integrates all things light and dark and I eventually developed the ability to be discerning as opposed to being judgmental.

Discernment is when you can see the aspects of something without attaching an emotion to it. We simply see what the difference is between one thing and another and make a choice. Judging happens when there is an emotion we assign to the things we are comparing.

Regarding judging, it is very important to me that you realize a pursuit of pureness doesn't make one person better than another or morally superior. This is genuinely about fostering that new Son energy and reducing the toxicity in your life.

The interesting thing about the distortion of naivety is that it is related to having a sense of wonder, which is part of the Son ideal I discuss in the next chapter.

Rider Reminders

- Always remember that you can hit the reset button.
- Being pure doesn't have to be about morality. You can focus on what you are consuming—the food, the water, the media, people in your life, your thoughts, your intentions, and how you talk to yourself.
- When the chips are down you can always tap into good memories and this will change your mood.

Chapter Two—Ask the Next Question

"He who can no longer pause to wonder and stand rapt in awe, is as good as dead; his eyes are closed." —Albert Einstein [4]

Son Ideal Number Two - Wonderment

A sense of wonder is similar to purity. The big difference is that purity is about the unadulterated newness of something, and wonderment has to do with our curiosity and willingness to learn. Sadly, we lose our sense of awe as we age. We start thinking we have figured things out. We *understand* things, so we think. We become content with what we know and run out of new things to discover. One of the cool things about the Son Wake Rider is how he is always open to learning and actively looks for new things to get excited about. He eagerly paddles out to the wakes with excitement and anticipates a mind-blowing ride. He treats life like an adventure and investigates new things. Engaging in a new skill can enrich the Son's experience. This is *not* an age thing. I totally feel we can have this sense of wonder at any stage of our life! We can be open to receiving new insights and enjoy new experiences which can result in an extraordinary life.

Astronomy comes to mind as something which gives me a sense of wonder. It is fascinating to look at the constellations on a dark night and wonder about the millions of stars and galaxies, and how they inspired so many people in the past. It is interesting to think about how space goes on and on and how there are billions of celestial bodies beyond what our eyes can see.

Knowing a bit about astronomy has also caused me to have an interest in Astrology. I love studying people and when I find out what their sign is, it is fascinating to connect the dots between their sign and personality traits.

Children are open to new ideas without being skeptical or having preconceived notions on how things are supposed to be. As adults, we can also be open and willing to go with the flow. It is great when we can be okay with not having answers right away and allowing things to naturally unfold.

We can give ourselves space and time to contemplate our thoughts, study new topics, and go on an inner journey. Or we can choose to be cut off from miracles and magic because we are caught up in how we think things are supposed to be. Most people struggle with having a sense of wonder because life is so massive that they are blinded by the vastness of the unknown.

I make my living doing creative work for small businesses. I place a high value on the freedom and flexibility I get from being my own boss. I have a process I follow when I develop and design things for customers. I seemed to have figured out a way to allow a ton of ideas to flow. The cool thing is that a lot of the mistakes I make often end up being better than my original idea. When this happens, it feels like magic and like I'm connected to a higher source of creativity beyond myself. I recently began calling this a *spiritual interrupt.*

I don't really understand how those wondrous interrupts and redirects happen, but it seems to be related to how all things are in perpetual motion and always changing. It is important to me to be open to change because it is one of the constants in life. If we can get to a place where we realize everything is always evolving, we can stop judging and being consumed with thoughts like "this is better" and "she's wrong" and "this is how it's going to be."

It's like the lyrics from one of my favorite Van Halen songs - "...*Change, nothin stays the same. Unchained and ya hit the ground running...*"

You get to decide how you are going to ride the wake! Take whatever life is going to throw at you and hit the ground running dude!

Son Distortion Number Three—Believing You Are Dumb

There are two distortions of the ideal of wonder. One of the extremes is when someone does not have the confidence to learn new things and they don't even try. They go through life having the same experiences over and over. People like this say "I'm just a simple person," "I'm not smart enough" and I'll never figure this out." You ask them how it's going and they say, "same ol same o." When they unconsciously judge themself as being dumb and use this type of self-talk, they just go through the motions and are not willing to learn because someone said they were dumb and they believed it.

This is kind of sad in my opinion, but I get it. The idea of staying content and safe in your comfort zone is so tempting and not a bad thing, but beating yourself up because you feel dumb is no Bueno. The fact of the matter is that we live in a very conventional society with social *norms* and aptitude tests are thrust upon kids. As hard as they try not to, these tests pigeonhole some kids into thinking they are dumb or learning disabled. The fact of the matter is that everyone has a unique way of learning. Everyone has their own way in which their genius shows up. Sadly, the educational authorities haven't figured out ways to take into account individual talents because they are too busy trying to figure out what is *normal* and what are the standard ways to test and measure the norms.

What I Did Before

Struggling to learn is not a foreign concept to me. I got decent grades in school but really had to work hard to get them. I had trouble comprehending things and often had to read things over and over, or really slow to understand what was being said. This made taking tests hard, especially when most of the kids in the class finished a lot quicker than me. I started worrying about looking dumb in front of everyone because I was usually one of the last ones to finish a test. I was not clever enough at the time to act like I was just being thorough.

Growing up I had this belief that I must've been kind of dumb and pondered why some kids just had a knack of learning and picking up things quicker than me. The problem with feeling dumb as a child is that it can really rob you of your confidence throughout your life. A lack of confidence can have a major impact on what we can achieve in life.

What I Do Now

It occurs to me now that I spent a lot of my childhood in an imaginary world. Some psychologists talk about kids spending the first five to six years of their life in a dreamlike state where the mind is often in delta or theta brainwave patterns. I imagine I was in an altered reality a lot back then and I actually work with these states in my creative process as an adult. I accept this about myself and just know it was part of my development.

Accepting the unique way you do things is the first step toward building confidence. I think the big lesson regarding feeling dumb has to do with trusting ourself and not worrying about what other people think of us. When we can take the pressure to perform away, learning becomes easier.

Regardless of what gurus you seek or how many books you read, if you think you are dumb or are full of negative self-talk, you are going to have a super hard time achieving your dreams. On our journey to becoming a whole dude, it is important to be aware of what we think about ourselves and the self-talk we use. So yeah, who cares if I had learning struggles as a kid, it has nothing to do with my worth as a person. I now believe, no matter what my learning style is, I have within me the capacity to solve any challenge I face, and this is all that really matters. I know this because throughout my life I have seen I can learn through doing and experimenting. I might not understand something at first but when I set time aside to dig into something and use trial and error, I do learn new skills because of the *doingness* and the willingness to try.

Learning new stuff can be sloppy and unrefined and most of my skills started out a bit raw. I now realize my sense of wonder regarding how things work is one way I tap into the infinite. My guitar playing, graphic designs, writing, video, and movie ideas can all start out sloppy and unrefined, but being open to new projects is very exciting to me. The pursuit is what excites me and along the way I don't have to worry about if I look dumb or not.

The old tape I used to play in my head was "I'm pretty good at a lot of things, but not great at anything." This doesn't matter to me anymore. The *jack of all trades master of none* inner dialogue isn't demoralizing me as it once was. I replaced it with "I'm pretty damn good at a lot of things and becoming exceptional at the skills I choose to focus on." Also, I know it's okay if I'm not the best at something. I know revision (re-vision) is part of the creative process and is a profound concept all of its own. I am constantly refining my work and that's half the fun.

A great way to end this part of the chapter is to share something I heard Steve Jobs, the co-founder of Apple say during an interview when he was talking about the early days of Apple. He made a comment about when we are growing up, we tend to think we have our place in the world and we just kind of accept how things are going to be. And then he said this magnificent thing I completely love:

"Life can be much broader once you discover this one simple fact - everything around you that you call life was made up by people no smarter than you, and you can change it and you can influence it and you can build your own things that other people can use."

Son Distortion Number Four—Being a Know it All

Science is interesting in that there are all these laws and rules which eventually get debunked. People thought the Earth was flat and this was proven wrong, and at one point they thought the Earth was the middle of the Universe and then Copernicus proved this was wrong when he distributed his theories about the Cosmos from his deathbed.

Then John Dalton developed the theory of atoms. Everyone believed him for a long time until it was discovered atoms were not the smallest thing and weren't even solid. Scientists eventually discovered even smaller atomic matter like quarks and then they found out the middle was nothing but energy. And so, there isn't a solid little building block after all.

Something more recent related to debunked scientific theories had to do with the Human Genome Project. The assumption was that the more evolved a species is it would have more genes than a less evolved species. When they discovered a fruit fly had around 25,000 genes it was assumed humans would surely have hundreds of thousands of genes. Eventually, they found out we did not have many more genes than a fruit fly. Everybody was blown away by the discovery.

My point is this, things as sanctimonious and institutionalized as scientific laws get debunked all the time—so it's okay to sit back and wonder how concrete stuff really is. A sense of wonderment is such a fantastic attribute of children because it opens them up to unlimited possibilities.

Not knowing the absolute answer to a question is truly a powerful way of being because it allows us to expand and grow.

The opposite of wonderment is when someone is being a know-it-all. What exactly is a know-it-all? I feel like when we reach a certain age, we think we've been around the block, seen a lot, and we think we know how everything works. We might even think we are experts at certain topics. We tend to not be open to learning new things and we cling to our need to be right. Our reality is so locked in, that we do not ever realize other alternatives exist. And then when we pick a side of an issue...*you know, the right side*, we must convince others we are right. It becomes a battle of egos.

What I Did Before

One day I read somewhere that if you can be right 51% of the time you are ahead of the game. When I read this I laughed at the idea and thought to myself, "Oh my gosh, I'm right *waaaay* more than 51% of the time!" I proceeded to calculate a few scenarios in my head and figured I was right probably 80–84% of the time. I find the fact that I ran a calculation estimating how right I am hysterical now.

I had this deep-seated desire to appear intellectual and show off how smart I was. When I think about my young adulthood now, I know this was probably a byproduct of my "Dumb Stupid David" belief system. I suppose for many years I had to prove to everyone I wasn't dumb. It's regrettable now to think about how much anxiety and energy went into this behavior. It takes a lot of work to prove you're right all the time. I must have come across as a bit cocky when I talked to people about art, music, wine, and quantum physics. Combining this with not understanding people's boundaries, I suppose I must have come across as a real tool.

What I Do Now

And then somehow I discovered *I don't always have to be right!* This has got to be one of the top ten days in my life! I realized other people have different perspectives than mine, and they have a lot to contribute as well. By being open to others' ideas, I grow tremendously. I realized my value as a person is not tied to how right I am. The older I get, the more I realize how little I know. (That or I really have forgotten *a lot.*) On the contrary, I think it is healthy to analyze my beliefs and as I say to a lot of people, "ask the next question."

Not having to be right all the time really leads you to be the most authentic version of yourself. A great practice to get into is if someone asks you a question and you don't know the answer simply say, "Wow that's a great question I'll have to wonder about that and get back to you." This willingness to not have to be right is the foundation of our next Wake Rider ideal which is honesty.

Rider Reminders

- We can be childlike and realize there are mysterious things that happen that are beyond our wildest imagination.
- *Facts* are debunked all the time.
- Being open-minded is a healthy way to feel and helps us connect to others.
- Ask the next question.

Chapter Three—From the Mouths of Babes

"Being honest may not get you a lot of friends but it'll always get you the right ones."
—John Lennon [5]

Son Ideal Number Three—Honesty

Hearing someone say they don't know the answer to something but will get back to you, is actually pretty refreshing. I feel like saying to these people, "Thanks for not telling me some ridiculous made-up answer." Knowing where I stand with someone and being on the same page is becoming something I value more and more in my life. This ideal is a root characteristic at the foundation for all the Wake Riders. It illustrates the best way to conduct ourselves and is the basis of building trustworthiness and character.

As adults, we often create a gray area around being honest. Everyone should be able to trust each other and be honest and open but that hardly happens and this results in us having trust issues and skepticism.

There is a lot of practicality to being honest, though. As they say, "honesty is the best policy." If you think about small children, they do not have any sort of filter going on when they say things. What comes out of the mouths of babes cracks me up. They just blurt stuff out as they see and feel things. It's beautiful to witness. They say stuff like: "Mommy, why is that old lady's hair blue?" or "Daddy! Look how that doggie is climbing on top of the other doggie."

What I Did Before

I was not always perfectly honest. One of the ways I've been dishonest was by hiding things out of fear. I spent most of the end of my marriage withholding information from my wife because I was afraid of what would happen if she knew the truth. I think my need to be likable and the need to always be in a peaceful environment also contributed to these less than honest episodes in my marriage. What made matters worse was how she would eventually find out about stuff and man what a mess that would make. You would think I would have learned.

One particular charade I pulled off for a couple of years was the re-emergence of playing and writing music. In what my ex-wife thought would be a motivating move, she brought up one of my old guitars from the basement to *decorate* my home office. She told me the guitar looked cool and might motivate me to work more. I'm not quite sure of the logic behind this. Being the rebel that I am, I decided to start writing songs and playing my guitar behind her back. I figured she'd be mad at me for wasting my time doing something so frivolous, and I hid my guitar playing from her. I wrote enough material to do an entire album. This was actually a pretty therapeutic activity that kept my emotions in check at the time.

I recorded a handful of the songs from back then and if I ever produce this album, I'm going to call it *Hidden* because they're all the songs that I hid from my wife. I did eventually tell my ex about all this a couple of years after our divorce, and I played her one of the songs I wrote called "Scorpio Moon."

She thought it was pretty cool.

What I Do Now

I don't feel the need to hide things from people anymore. I've figured out how to be brave enough to just bite the bullet and let people know what is going on inside my head. But I'm careful how I tell people my truth.

I think one of the key things to mention about honesty is how people deliver information. Some people are brutally honest and almost hurtful with the things they say and have no regard for people's feelings. Some people are the extreme opposite—they're so afraid of being disliked (or so frightened by confrontation) that they omit information or use inventive language because they don't want to hurt people's feelings.

Then there are people who are petrified of what they think will happen if the truth is known. They become habitual liars out of their need for protection. While some people can be brash when they are being honest, others have a knack for being sincere and graceful when they speak. They have a way of softening the blow when they deliver bad news. My Mom is a good example of this type of person. She has a tendency of expressing her concern with my appearance at times since she comes from a generation where being dressed dapper was important. She has a really sweet way of expressing her concern and I know it is coming from a place of love. She has a very angelic quality about her and so it is kind of funny to watch her voice her lack of approval but she does it without ruffling anyone's feathers.

I realize now how important it is to be honest and to not create gray areas with people. As a result, my communication with others is much more clear and agreements that are made are easier to keep.

Son Distortion Number Five—Lies to Self

One might say there is only one extreme opposite of being honest and this is being dishonest, but for the sake of this discussion, I'm saying there are two ways of being dishonest. These two versions are when you are dishonest to others and when you are dishonest with yourself. Both are behaviors that come from a place of fear. I think lying to ourselves is a huge problem because we literally shape our reality by our thoughts and internal dialogue. One big way lying to ourselves shows up is through denial.

What I Did Before

I've spent a bit of my life in denial about having type two diabetes. I want to be upfront about this because I don't want to sound hypocritical. It's challenging at times because I'm trying to manage it naturally. It is tricky because I don't want to *be* the diagnosis. My feeling is that my mindset, emotional state, and choices should be focused on moving me toward wellness and not just constantly thinking about my *disease*.

Western/Allopathic medicine, in my opinion, seems to be always looking back at illness and its symptoms versus being proactive and doing things to move you toward wellness. There is obviously a lot of benefit due to all the advances in medicine, but I consider this to be acute care versus preventative care, as it doesn't seem to address the root of the root of the root of the problem.

In my opinion, I'm walking a fine line between being reckless and in denial about my health compared to taking responsibility for my actions. I believe in the power of my mind and my ability to heal myself. At the same time I know my life is affected by my behaviors and the damage my decisions can cause. It is easy for me to be dishonest with myself and not take this situation seriously or pretend that it isn't an issue.

What I Do Now

I think we are not honest with ourselves out of fear. This could be centered around our health concerns or maybe worries related to our finances. We choose to think ignorance is bliss sometimes. Instead of being brave enough to face reality, it's easier to just keep our heads in the sand and not think about things. We create diversions so we don't have to face our current circumstances. If we are not careful though, this behavior can backfire and be damaging in the long run.

I try to check in with where I am at with each of these fear-inducing situations one at a time. When I get an idea of where I am at with a health challenge I can come up with a way to focus solely on what is in front of me. I can make a realistic plan and be proactive, be accountable, and be in action heading to where I want to be. When I drop the self-judgment, it makes room for me to adjust my behavior and be honest with myself. I think this practical approach can be helpful and less anxiety-inducing. It isn't always easy, but I think it is worth it in the long run. I discuss managing fears more in Chapter five and those are the strategies I am implementing now versus being in denial.

Son Distortion Number Six—Lies to Others

Lying to other people is about being afraid of what the outcome is going to happen if we tell the truth. If this becomes a habit, the lines of our reality get blurred. It's one of these things that when we do it over and over and over it just gets easier to do and it turns into a behavior and potentially etches in stone our character. I think we all fib a little. I know I do sometimes. At the very least I tell little half-lies to just keep the peace at times. But like I said, it's rooted in fear and that is not being whole.

I don't have as much fear around people's reaction to what I say anymore. I'm not an insensitive jerk, mind you. What I'm saying is that I don't put myself into such an anxious state where I feel I have to stretch the truth.

There is a gray area people tap dance around and don't technically lie but are deceitful due to withholding information. I had a very serious girlfriend after my divorce who fell into this category. She was really a quite lovely woman but was so worried about what people thought of her. Even though she really, really wanted to be honest and liked by people, when she got into compromising situations, she just left out details and stayed in that gray area. Her behavior got caught a few too many times and she lost close friends over it (including me).

Another thing to mention is that most people can sense when they are being lied to. I've been this way all of my life—since I'm very sensitive to people's energy—even to the degree where I even questioned authority figures and their authenticity.

In addition to being mindful of the words we choose, it is important that we are aware of the intention behind what we say. Remember, everything is energy. The words we speak are energy, and the thoughts we have even before we speak are energy. Some of us can sense this energy behind people's words. People can say one thing, but the energy and intention speak even louder than their words. Let's just say this can be picked up on, and it's best when the intention matches up with the words if you are trying to come from a place of pure honesty.

So remember, be brave and tell the truth! It is all in your delivery. One way to soften the blow when sharing bad news is to use humor. Make people laugh. And this is the perfect segue into the final Son Wake Rider's ideal, which is about being fun.

Rider Reminders

- The foundation of your character begins with honesty.
- It isn't always easy to be honest, but try not to get in the habit of lying too much because it can really impact your reality.
- Be mindful of how you deliver information to people. Try to be direct but not too harsh. Be sensitive to the other person's feelings when you deliver the news.

Chapter Four—Boys... Just Wanna Have Fun

"Do anything, but let it produce joy." -Walt Whitman [6]

Son Ideal Number Four—Fun

The Son Wake Rider thrives on having fun. He gives himself permission to lighten up a little and enjoy himself. He takes the time off to sneak out to the ocean to surf because he knows there may not be a tomorrow.

What's the point of having a life if you aren't having fun?

I picked this as a Son ideal to remind people to have a look at how they are living their life. Have you become a dull person so caught up in your career that there is no adventure or anything fun to look forward to? We can get lost in our daily routines and our life becomes mundane. It's like a march to the grave. Think about this and evaluate your fun quotient.

Are you stuck on autopilot a little too much?

At any given moment, we can infuse some fun into our life if we just remember to give ourselves permission to cut loose. Having a sense of humor and being able to laugh is a big part of the equation, and it's quite astounding to think about how little time we spend genuinely laughing.

A few nights ago, I was having a hard time sleeping because I had some aches and pains I was dealing with. It was 3:00 in the morning and I realized probably the only thing that would distract me from the pain would be some laughter. I googled Robin Williams and found an hour and a half long show he did in 2012 on Broadway. Holy cow, what a riot! The guy was a wild man. I laughed my butt off. You can tell it was a totally different era of comedy then. He just didn't care about ethnic sensitivity, or he was in such a state of flow he didn't realize what was even coming out of his mouth. 80% of everything he said probably would have been offensive to someone, but he was amazing with his delivery and the crowd roared with laughter the entire show.

Robin Williams was so spontaneous and in the moment. I think we can all take a page out of his book when it comes to being fun. I think sometimes we just have to let it rip and not worry about what people think. I'm not saying to be racially inappropriate; I am saying we shouldn't be so petrified in our fear of worrying about what people think and allowing this to rob us of the opportunity to have fun.

Whether it's our attempt at humor, or how we look on the dance floor at a wedding, or when a friend pulls us up on stage to sing karaoke, we need to just live in the moment and not give a crap about what others think of us and just go for it! *Pura Vida!* But as men, we are not taught to act this way and we aren't supposed to look foolish.

We get so busy with all our responsibilities as adults, we forget we are on earth to experience joy and excitement in our life. Having structure and positive habits is all fine and good and helpful, but if we do not have enough time or flexibility, life does not feel very fun. Before we know it, we are in our late 40's, or worse yet our 50's, scratching our head and saying to ourselves, "Where did my life go?"

Every year I have a group of guys with whom I go on an NGA weekend trip. NGA = No Girls Allowed. This is the one weekend a year we take the time to let our hair down (what's left of it) and not worry about anything. We play poker, goof off, and eat and drink whatever we want. Usually, we play a round of golf.

I'm not a golfer and the *only* time I ever do is during these trips. I used to worry about how terrible I'd play because most of my buddies hit the links on a regular basis.

The first few years I was miserable and super self-conscious of every single golf swing I took and would cringe if I would screw-up. I feared I was slowing everyone down, and that I looked like that buffoon in *Caddyshack*. You remember the guy who takes a hundred strokes and is cussing on every hole.

Then one year I was sitting in the golf cart and it was a gorgeous November day. The temperature was perfect, and the sky was a deep shade of blue. I was smoking a cigar with my buddy Mike. "This is the *best* day ever!" I thought to myself. "Look at this, you get to goof off with your lifelong buddies on a beautiful day chasing a little white ball around." I realized then I was blessed to be able to afford such a trip and to have the flexibility to take the time away from my work. I was totally blissed out and made up my mind that I would always enjoy our little golf outing regardless of how bad I played. As a result of this emotional shift, I totally took the pressure off myself and started improving my game, and made decent shots from time to time which added even more fun to the situation.

Life is all about squeezing as much juice out of it as we can before we are six feet underground. Stay present as often as you can, and this will indirectly increase the joy in your life.

Another thing related to our fun quotient is creativity. If you think of kids, you'll remember most of them are little artists and have incredible imaginations. I recommend you consider trying a new artistic endeavor. It is truly therapeutic to do creative things. It could be a fun new activity you do just for yourself. Whether it's spending time listening to music or even learning how to play a musical instrument, having something creative in your life can have a very healing effect. When we do creative things there's a sense of timelessness that gives the logical part of our brain a rest. A lot of our daily stress gets abated because of this. Also, it's always great to have something coming up to look forward to.

Set the intention now to add an activity you can do on a regular basis that adds creativity to your life.

Son Distortion Number Seven—Dull

I suspect part of the reason people are dull or afraid of doing fun stuff is that they may be shy or they may want to avoid being caught looking silly or incompetent. Or maybe they fear that they will somehow be thought of as being uncouth. On the surface, this is an issue related to shame. It can even take years to have this breakthrough because of all of our social conditioning.

It's also important to not be afraid of messing up when you try something new. Give yourself permission to fail early and often. We can put a lot of pressure on ourselves trying to do everything perfectly. The older I get the more I realize there really is no such thing as failure and there's no reason to feel bad about trying something new. I do think some people are so afraid of being humiliated they are petrified by the thought of trying something new or doing something fun and whimsical. After years and years of this behavior, they just turn into dull people stuck in their comfort zone.

What I Did Before

The height of my shyness probably came between ninth and eleventh grade. This was a result of going to three different schools within three years. I went to a private Catholic grade school from second through eighth grade and essentially hung around the same twenty or so classmates for seven years. I came from a large Catholic middle-class family and we all switched from private school in eighth grade to the public school system for our high school years. This was kind of rough on me because I was so close to my grade school friends and I was one of only a handful of kids who did not go on to a private high school.

Besides having to feel like I was one of the *poor kids* whose parents could not afford a private school education, I had to go to a new school where I didn't know anyone except a couple of kids from my street and a couple of kids from my grade school. This took place during my awkward teen years when it was so important to fit in and be accepted by my friends, and it resulted in my being very shy and terrified by the prospect of looking or doing anything weird.

I just wanted to fit in and be accepted. I had to pretend I was cool.

If I only knew then what I know now.

What I Do Now

Flash forward to the current day and I can confidently say I believe life is meant to be lived to the fullest and people shouldn't be afraid to try new things and have fun.

I think the remedy to being dull or shy is to push against your comfort zone. After you do this over and over again, you'll find you survive and most of those worst-case scenarios you have in your head never really come to fruition.

Also, I eventually figured out the emotions of shame, guilt, and shyness are completely worthless and limit the amount of joy, fun, and bliss I can have in my life.

Son Distortion Number Eight—Reckless

If one distortion of the fun ideal is essentially being afraid to have fun, what is the other extreme? You guessed it: Having *too much* fun, to the degree where you're reckless. I think there is a happy medium between having fun and not going to the extreme of living dangerously.

When the riptides are dangerous or severe storms are moving in, even the Son Wake Rider knows it's a bad idea to go out and surf.

What I Did Before

I cracked my head open eight times as a kid because I was so reckless in my *Dumb Stupid David* phase. This included busting a 7Up bottle on my head and falling out a second-story window, but this wasn't the worst of my reckless behavior as a kid.

As I'm editing these notes I'm sitting outside working on my laptop, and it is near Independence Day. There are a ton of fireworks going off in the background. It brings back memories of how much of a pyromaniac I was when I was a kid. Lighting off regular firecrackers and blowing stuff up just wasn't good enough for me.

One of my childhood hobbies was making model rockets, and at some point, I found out how amazing it was to ignite their engines, which were basically concentrated gunpowder. I used to break them up and light them on fire, and I loved to watch the big white flash and all the smoke—until the day one went off in my hand. I was lucky because one of my friend's Dad got home from work early and took me to my doctor's office. My hand was in such bad shape the doctor gave me some codeine and said I needed a plastic surgeon.

So off we went to the hospital, where a surgeon and my Mom were waiting for me (and thankfully not my Dad). I had two fingers melted together and most of the skin on my left hand was so charred the skin had to be cut off. For the next two or three months, my hand was bandaged and I had to sleep with it elevated because the throbbing was so bad. I still remember the cartoon my friend Mike drew of my burnt hand and me in a puff of smoke. He titled it "Burnt Peach" (for whatever reason Peach was my nickname back then). I'm still a bit of a pyro and like building bonfires, but I definitely don't play with gunpowder anymore.

Throughout my life, I've made my share of poor choices and have been a bit reckless. I have made poor financial decisions and have been known to party a little too much. I was reckless a few times in the past when I drove home after drinking booze. I never got *wasted* and drove mind you, but one of the reasons I'm a big believer in guardian angels is because there were many times in my young adult life I'm almost certain there was some form of divine intervention that helped me get home after a night of parties. Back then, my main focus was on having *fun-fun-fun,* and I showed very poor judgment. I don't drink much anymore because I don't like the depressive effect it has on me during the next couple of days, but this wasn't always the case.

I used to play on a Monday night hockey team and a group of us would have beers afterward. There was a night involving my foot hockey days I'll never forget. It took place the year the Cardinals played the Astros in the National League Championship Series. Albert Pujols crushed a home run off Brad Lidge and my buddies and I were blown away by his blast. In my opinion, I think Brad Lidge, who was a preeminent closer, took three or four years to get his stuff back after giving up that home run. We were very excited and celebrated, but thankfully I slowed my roll a little with the beers and just savored the moment.

For whatever reason on my drive home, I got the idea that I needed to stop for Ho-Hos. During my detour, what I thought was a blinking yellow was apparently a blinking red. As fate would have it, I was pulled over by a cop who proceeded to do every test in the book to check my sobriety. He looked at my eyes with his flashlight and did that finger thing, made me walk in a line, and even made me say the alphabet backward. My adrenaline was pulsing throughout my entire body to the point where I could feel my body shake. Any *buzz* I had from the booze was surely gone after all the field sobriety tests.

The cop said I seemed nervous and wanted to know why. I proceeded to tell him that I was driving a company vehicle and if anything should happen, I would probably lose my job. While he was a pretty nice guy, he was not overly sympathetic and ended up giving me a breathalyzer test anyway. Afterward, he was in his vehicle for what seemed like an eternity and I figured I was dead meat. I'm not sure if my guardian angels did their thing and messed with the meter, or if I was sober enough because of the adrenaline or all the time it took to do the field testing, or if the cop was just being cool, but when he came back to my car, he said I could go and to drive safely. I said thank you and drove straight home (sans the Ho-Hos).

What I Do Now

Part of being reckless involves not paying attention. I now strive to make every single day count and I try to stay present as often as I can. I remind myself to slow down and cherish the moment, and that there's no need to rush. I'm also trying to get a little more structure in my life. I will talk about this more in the Warrior section in chapter six.

A big part of the Son's reckless behavior stems from wanting to rebel. The Son begins to realize the system is flawed and he doesn't want to believe in a lot of the things he did as a small boy anymore. Having fun is one thing and is ideal, but when we get too attached to our desires, it can result in destructive behavior. The Son's rebellion can oddly turn into a good quality of the Warrior and this is where the next section of the book starts off.

Rider Reminders

- Don't become boring but don't be too reckless or irresponsible.
- Laugh more
- Don't worry about what other people think of you.
- Don't play with gunpowder
- Do something creative

Son Section Takeaways

The First B Word—Beliefs

When I thought of the concept of having a *B Word*, the intention was to come up with one word you could remember a particular Wake Rider by. Something that encapsulated all of his qualities and acted as an anchor to help you remember the lessons he learns. The word *beliefs* quickly came to mind as the Son's B Word because if we are going to embark on a journey of growth and change, questioning our beliefs seems like a great way to start.

You didn't pick your parents, your teachers, or the religion you followed as a child. And as you were growing up you didn't have much say on who influenced you. As kids, we just wanted to be recognized and to fit in.

When I showed up to second grade as the new city kid in blue corduroy pants, little did I know this would be the origins of my moral compass. As if through osmosis, I learned about what was appropriate and what wasn't.

After saying "Hi" to my eventual best man Brian while I made my way to the desks in the back row, I noticed *The Castle*. This larger-than-life cardboard structure sat in the back of Miss B's classroom and it housed the prince and princess for the day who got all the attention. They were *special*. On that particular day the prince was Matt Lanham and the princess was Mary Ann Gilliam.

All of Miss B's righteous beliefs and views of the world were gradually embedded into us second graders. We were introduced to the world of guilt and shame and these emotions were reinforced each day when it was revealed whether we earned the dreaded *Black X* or the coveted *Gold Star*. Miss B (bless her heart as they say in the south) became an influence on the way I processed the world and she inadvertently molded me into the conventional, rule-following, good Catholic boy I was supposed to be (until I wasn't).

In the movie *How to Lose a Guy in Ten Days,* Matthew McConaughey takes his girlfriend (played by Kate Hudson) to see his family on Staten Island, and as they walk into the house you hear people yelling "BUUULLSHIT!" It seems like something bad or possibly violent is going on, but then you hear a bunch of laughter. When they go back to the deck area where his family is, everyone is playing cards. They had a bunch of cards in their hands, and each person would declare what they were holding. The other players would guess whether the person was being honest or not. If they thought the person was lying, they'd yell "BUUULLLSHIT!"

What does all of this have to do with beliefs you may ask? As I got older I started to understand this is how our beliefs work. Just like that card game, we eventually get to pick and choose what kind of BUUULLLSHIT we want to believe (and have others believe about us).

Einstein said that you can't solve a problem with the same consciousness level that created it. In order to evolve, you need to maintain a childlike sense of wonder and begin to question everything.

We are at a point in history where all of the old systems should be challenged. The world is so fractured now, it feels like everything is ready to crumble. It's time to question our values, our biases, and prejudices. Time to question concepts such as inclusion versus exclusivity. It's time to review who our role models are and what they represent to us—Are they flawed and outdated?

Also, it's important to me to make the point that everyone gets to have their own beliefs. Not one person is more right than the next person in my opinion. They just have their unique perspective and what they feel is true. Here's the deal: We all have free will. We all decide what we want to believe and how we're going to ride the wakes as they arise in our lives. We get to decide what works for us based on our current circumstances and past experiences.

Many, many, *many* people try to search for the truth and want to base their beliefs off of this truth. In my opinion, this search is futile because the entire Universe is in a constant state of movement. Something that may have appeared true ends up getting debunked. I feel strongly now that I'd rather put the energy I previously spent seeking truth into pursuing being the purest version of myself as possible instead.

The bottom line is this: try to figure out what BUUULLLSHIT you want to believe in and what you don't because it's all BUUULLLSHIT!

Rite of Passage

Evolved people use pain as a signal to be introspective and to learn and grow. Eventually when we are in enough pain we can lean into it and try to figure out what the lesson is. Each time this happens I feel we move into the next phase of development.

We often think a rite of passage that boys go through to become a man. We picture some sort of ritual that we are supposed to go through like a young brave in a Native American tribe hanging by hooks in a great lodge. Or it might be sexual, like when we lose our virginity and then like in the movies we then magically become a real man because this clumsy act.

As I reflected on my life, I realized that I've had more than one rite of passage.. I bring this up because it seems like the idea of a rite of passage seems to have disappeared from our Western culture. It's important to point out the different types of rites of passage we face as men as we grow and evolve. We are not one and done.

The Son's Rite of Passage happens when it becomes very clear to him that there are the haves and have-nots. This causes a loss of innocence at a psychological level because he begins to feel unworthy and forgets to remember he is whole already and is good enough just as he is. At this stage of development, an illusion around the need for acceptance by others is born, and an entire lifetime can be tainted by this very real and draining need.

As young people, we took on other's beliefs because of our need for approval and attention. What complicates the situation even more is that we live in a society that tells us we need to *fit in* and at the same time asserts *membership has its privileges.*

We are tricked into having conditional worthiness based on things outside of ourselves.

Corporations capitalize on this by turning us into materialistic people who think we need to dress a certain way or listen to certain music to be cool and liked. Then the sense of separation grows even more when we think about the *in-crowd*, the *winners*, and how we can't go certain places because access is reserved for members only.

Society uses possessions and comparing ourselves to others as a way to keep us trapped.

We live in a LAME culture. LAME = Look At Me. We use Instagram filters to make wrinkles disappear so we can admire our fake image that match pictures of airbrushed celebrities.

So what happened to that innocent child full of wonder and daydreams who doesn't judge people? Ultimately, the pain and hurt from a sense of not being good enough gives birth to the foundational desire of the Warrior.

Exercise

My intention for the exercises at the end of each section is for these new thoughts to take root and help you grow. Hopefully, they can help you uncover memories or traumas that are stuck inside of you that need to be processed and released. If you want to go deeper, I have a video course available for each Wake Rider intended to help you explore further if you like.

But for now, what is something you regret about your childhood? Was it an event that happened or perhaps something you wanted and never got? Journal about this.

PART TWO - The Warrior

The Whole Dude

The Warrior Wake Rider
Victim to Victor

> *"I have learned that success is to be measured not so much by the position that one has reached in life as by the obstacles which he has overcome while trying to succeed.—Booker T. Washington* [7]

The Warrior's Journey

At the end of the previous section, we discussed how the Son's *loss of innocence* leaves him feeling hurt and reckless. This pain is what expands the Son into the immature version of the Warrior as he develops the skills to go from victim to victor. He goes from feeling scared and unprotected to making others feel safe and providing protection for them.

This section is about the achiever that is in every one of us. We are socially conditioned to have a drive to succeed and this almost unequivocally is the brush that paints most people's reality. There is a conventional blueprint laid out that has been passed down from generation to generation.

The hero's journey has been told to us through hundreds of stories. My intention of this section is to go deeper and discuss some of the nuances that are related to being an achiever, especially since life often isn't always perfect and it's good to have something to ponder when it's not.

It's one thing to read a book and get coaching; it's another thing to practice and apply what you learn. No matter how many times a huge wake knocks the Warrior off his surfboard, he climbs back on and has the audacity to try again.

And each time he does, he gets a little stronger and creates the muscle memory to be a little better. He understands *true* strength comes from controlling his emotions and sharpening his wits—which is equally as important as developing the physical muscles needed to succeed. He ultimately figures out how he can harness and direct energy in any given moment.

The Warrior's Desire

The Son's desire to be recognized progresses to become the Warrior's root desire to be *victorious.* This drive for victory stems from the Son's pain of needing to be accepted. He feels if he can win he will be able join the members-only crowd.

The extreme version of this desire is the need to win at all costs. Being competitive seems to be wired into men's DNA. In ancient days, a young man went to battle not only to protect his people but also enjoy the spoils of victory.

This primal urge to conquer is still inside of men. We aren't necessarily worried about being attacked by a pack of wolves or an enemy tribe torching our camp, but we are also only seven or eight generations away from that way of life. The modern-day version of this warrior energy might well up in our gut when we show up on the football field competing against our crosstown rival, or it could cause the pounding in our heart when we are competing in a sales contest at work.

We want to win, dammit!

While there is nothing wrong with this. Like all desires, if they can inspire us without getting distorted, they are healthy and natural. Also, I think the four Warrior ideals that stem from his desire are essential building blocks needed on our path to fulfilling our potential.

Why This Is Important

I can't count the number of years I wasted in victim mode. Opportunities to have joy in my life were distorted by the lens of a victim. Honestly, it really sucks when I think about it. Numerous relationships were tainted by victim stories I told as well as not being fully present during what should have been major highlights of my life. Thank goodness I've *done the work* and can quickly recognize if I'm slipping into feeling like a victim.

Our culture is so attached to the concept of winning. Billions of dollars are spent on sports because of the high we each experience when our team wins. It almost seems unnatural how important winning is to us. Most of us equate our value as a man to our number of wins and losses. We count the physical things in our life that we accumulate as trophies commemorating all our victories. But when you're on your deathbed, those prizes won't mean shit.

Another thing to consider that's related to this over-aggressive nature is the amount of violence in the world. Young men are often numb to it because of its pervasiveness in movies and video games. Kids get a rush from playing violent video games, and It seems like there is some sort of bloodlust lurking within young men (I'd love to see a study on how our body's chemistry changes during a video simulation).

Narcissistic, self-important behavior and "it's not my problem" attitudes seem to rule these days. I feel like this has the potential of inciting violence, riots, and cataclysmic events. It feels like we live in a time where our divided views and lack of respect for one another might cause a civil war. All the hate and intolerance is scary in my opinion.

These behaviors I feel result in hardness and lack of flexibility. Men seem to be turning brittle and losing their heart connection in the process. I think the result of this behavior results in losing out on a lot of joy and sweetness throughout our life. And frankly I believe it can also make our bones brittle, our muscles stiff, and our heart clogged. My point is that our beliefs and behaviors can truly manifest as physical disease in our body.

Who Comes to Mind When I Think of the Warrior Wake Rider

Two people come to mind when I think of the Warrior. Tom Cruise's character Captain Nathan Algren in *The Last*

Samurai and Pat Morita's character Mr. Miyagi in *The Karate Kid*. Despite being a veteran of both the U.S. Civil War and Indian War, Captain Algren is an example of the immature Warrior, who is learning the skills of the Samurai and developing the mental and emotional discipline of a true warrior..

Mr. Miyagi, on the other hand, I see as the mature Warrior. He has already put in the work to hone his skills. He has been battle tested and has accomplished great things. He is very patient and understands the value in being diplomatic. He has the calmness and presence of mind to know going to battle is the last resort.

The Warrior's Core Strength

The Warrior has the determination to push through tough times and has the discipline and drive to succeed. This Warrior energy comes from the passion he has from being excited about what he is doing at any given moment.

We can tap into this energy to develop our prowess on a physical level, but it's important to realize we are more than biochemical beings. Where does this drive originate? It is this initial invisible rage inside the Warrior that makes him feel dissatisfied. It is this CORE RAGE we experience when we want changes in our life. This initial spark eventually turns into the fire we need to push us forward to get after it to pursue what we want to achieve. Hence the core strength of the Warrior Wake Rider is courage because it is at the root of what drives all his ideal behaviors.

Gonna Fly Now

My first memory of experiencing Warrior energy was the summer the movie *Rocky* was playing in theaters. I think it was around 1976. Can you think of any other character that personifies the grit and determination of Rocky Balboa?

That summer I was fully immersed in the excitement of being on my first swim team: The Westglen Polar Bears!

The irony is that a few summers prior to this I almost drowned during another *Dumb Stupid David* moment. My family was having a picnic at Springdale Pool. We still lived in the city, and this was one of the only times we went to a public pool. I don't remember a ton about this day, but for some reason, I can still hear Tommy James "Draggin' the Line" singing in the background on the radio. It was my first time at such a big pool, and I was excited to jump in and swim even though I had no clue what I was doing. Painted on the concrete in big white letters was "5 ft." I was just learning to read, and I recognized the number 5. My naive interpretation was that this is where the five-year-olds were supposed to swim. Without any thought, I jumped in and proceeded to go straight to the bottom of the pool. Thank God my brother Mike was nearby to pull me out.

I don't think I swam much after that Springdale episode. I never got swim lessons, and like so many things in my life, I learned the hard way, by being self-taught. Fast forward a few years, and it was a time when my parents needed to keep me busy on summer break, and they signed me up to join our neighborhood swim team.

There are two distinct things I remember about that summer related to the Warrior Wake Rider. The first thing I remember is how I came in last place in every race I was put in. No matter how hard I splashed and flopped around and kicked my butt off, I lost. I just didn't have the skills to win a race. The little warrior in me never gave up as I put my heart and soul into every single race. I showed up to every early morning practice and swam in the chilly 7:00 a.m. water. Hence the name Polar Bears.

The number one thing that kept me motivated to show up was our super cool coach, Jose. I discovered it felt good to be noticed and encouraged by him.

Jose was this kind of lanky guy who wore these round John Lennon glasses and resembled Peter Tork from The Monkees. He had a great way to get us kids excited to compete. He was really into *Rocky*. He fired us up before swim meets by playing "Gonna Fly Now" and we'd run out on the pool deck waving our arms up above our heads. When he blew the whistle we dropped down and did one armed push-ups just like Rocky.

One super sweet memory about how I really got hooked happened when my coach drove me to an away swim meet. He had this purple Javelin convertible. I remember going down the road with the Rocky theme song playing and Jose had the top down. The wind was blowing in my face and I was waving my arm with the wind. It literally felt like I was flying. Magic!

Even though I didn't really know what I was doing and had terrible technique, I had this very *raw* drive to give it my best. I pushed and pushed and was exhausted after every race. Then the most incredible thing happened, and I knew I was going to come back the next summer. At the award ceremony at the end of the season, while all my teammates were getting ribbons and medals they earned in the championship meet, I just sat and watched. I didn't qualify to race in the big conference championship. Then something happened I will never forget. I got the last medal handed out. It was a gold medal presented in a little box and there was a little note which said: "Most dedicated." I was overwhelmed with pride when my Mom explained to me what it meant. Consequently, the next summer I started to win races.

I share this story to remind you that even though you don't always win it is important to stay dedicated to your craft and to continue to move towards targets that help you grow.

Chapter Five—Managing Monsters

"Courage is the most important of all the virtues because, without courage, you can't practice any other virtue consistently." —
Maya Angelou [8]

Warrior Ideal Number One—Courage

Do you have a favorite song you listen to that gets you pumped up? I have several but as I write this I have "You Can't Always Get What You Want" by the Rolling Stones blasting in the background. I get pretty jazzed listening to Mick and the boys croon this classic. I always have to shape my lips just like Jagger when I sing along. The funny thing is that the song is about being complacent. But man oh man, Mick is really trying to talk himself into believing everything will be okay.

If it wasn't for the very subtle hurt going on, I might not love the tune so much. There is a certain amount of pain we experience when we are complacent and just putting up with our life and things that we feel we can't change or we aren't motivated enough to do anything about. The only good thing about being hurt is that it can get us off our butt when the pain is too much to bear. When we finally get sick of feeling down, hurt, or disappointed, it turns into a bit of a core rage that can be put to use if we can leverage it and use it to take action. If we were just happy-go-lucky all the time we might miss out on this motivation.

This initial rage fuels the drive in us that ultimately grows into the discipline and grit we need to succeed. I think determination is a byproduct of the courage it sometimes takes to just get out of bed on rough mornings and get after it with a plan and a positive attitude.

It's important to me to go into depth regarding how courage shows up in our modern day-to-day lives. Even though we aren't on the battlefield fighting our enemies, there are many things that come up frequently that require it. In a nutshell, the Warrior's drive is about the side of us that wants to achieve goals and manifest great things. How we interact with people and the boundaries which may need to be created is a good example of leveraging courage. The choices we are forced to make each day, as well as our need to be true to ourselves, all require courage. When faced with tough situations, sometimes we cower and hide or we manipulate others if we are feeling wounded or weak, but eventually we can tap into that inner warrior's energy to take the first step toward the change we want.

I have a vision board hanging up in my bedroom that I created several years ago. It depicts what I wanted to accomplish and achieve. It also has little hand-written notes I made to myself. Eventually, I began pulling many of the pictures from it because I realized those images just represented *stuff* once important to me to acquire. Possessions like a vintage Fender Telecaster and the herb garden I wanted to grow in my backyard. All these things that seem ridiculous to me now like a Bentley in the driveway of a massive stone and brick house (twice the size of one I once built). If you look at it from a certain perspective, a vision board is a limited way of thinking. It is just stuff and for the most part, none of it really matters to me anymore.

After I took many of the pictures off the board, what remained were the little handwritten signs I made to myself. I had a little three-inch by three-inch sign which said *no fear* written in black marker. There were other notes including *self-love*, *give*, and *receive*. The *no fear* sign, while noble, didn't feel 100% right to me, and I eventually took it off. Mind you, I've had this vision board for over nine years.

A few months went by and I thought about how the unconscious mind works and how it doesn't process a negative. Basically, the *no fear* message was being heard at a deeper level as *fear*. This little sign was beaming at me the message *fear-fear-fear-fear-fear* on a subtle level, and I didn't even realize it. Ironically over the last six to seven years of my life, I've had a lot of fears showing up in my psyche. But I liked the *idea* of having no fear ... you know like, being in control of my circumstances where I'm not only not afraid, but I truly kick ass at whatever I do. I'm not saying push the envelope and be reckless, but when you are this bad ass you know you are going to be safe and succeed.

This idea of *no fear* seems to apply the most in the mental stuff that pops up in my head on a daily basis and I wanted to come up with a word that describes this characteristic better. I wanted a word to remind me of the alpha male energy that I wanted to be able to tap into every time I saw those words on my vision board. I wanted something to get me off my ass. Suddenly a vision of a tenacious hungry wolf came to mind. After having that mental image, I started using the word *courage*, and I made a new sign to stare at each morning when I first woke up.

There is no duality when it comes to the word courage. It is just a straightforward word. The word courage has all those *no fear* things and more! It is not only situational but also an ongoing mindset.

Hollywood gives us so many examples of what being fearless is supposed to look like. Anything from Mufasa from *The Lion King* to Mel Gibson in blue war paint in *Braveheart* to Rambo and any version of James Bond we've seen. A lot of that machismo simply doesn't feel real to me to be honest. There is so much symbolism in our culture around courage. You can visualize what courage looks like when you think of these characters and symbols. I don't think this is a bad thing, but I think courage is much greater than our physical abilities, as it comes into play in many other practical ways, and not just what you muster up for some pretend epic physical battle like a movie character.

Let's say you are a bit depressed or you have anxiety about the future, having courage is a great way to shift out of those temporary thoughts and emotions.

It takes courage to go deep and figure out what you value and to act on your convictions. Like being brave enough to ask your boss for a raise or telling your clients you are raising your rates. These actions can have a big economic impact on your life. What about having the capacity to speak up to an intimate partner or family member to tell them how you feel about a topic that has been too awkward to bring up? Think of the relief you will have once you get all those things out on the table. It may be painful to go through, but it will be worth it because you don't need to have all the internal strife and conflict anymore.

What if you've been isolated, and on your own, and lonely? Conjure up the drive to connect with people and socialize. It doesn't have to be anything big or elaborate. Just get out there. Or maybe the opposite is the case: you're in a hurtful relationship and you're staying around because you don't know what the future will bring or how you will survive on your own. Consider taking the first steps of moving on or at least start the dialogue with your partner and be honest regarding your feelings.

When we're fed up with our circumstances, having core rage helps us remember who we are and that being whole is our default setting.

Warrior Distortion Number One—Fearful

What is the opposite of courage? The obvious answer is fear. It's important to talk about fear because we live in a world that seems to be completely run by fear. Mass media thrives at continuing this messaging because fear sells and consumes people's attention. Being able to discern if something is a legitimate fear or not is critical.

There are very real things that can pop up suddenly which might cause a fright, like if you are driving down the highway and your tire blows out, or if you're on a float trip and you suddenly see a big black snake swimming right at your tube and you can't remember which snakes are venomous and which aren't. Those are legit reasons to have some panic and have the fight or flight reflex kick in.

Unfortunately, we can go through life with unreasonable fears which are just thoughts in our head. I call these our self-created monsters. Sadly, our unconscious mind doesn't really know the difference between a real-life threat or something made up. In the long run, we can suffer health consequences if we are constantly in a state of fear. I feel the more we can be aware of how our emotions work, the more we can see how everything connects and affects how we feel.

One belief I hold is that fears are never fully going to go away because they are related to our ego trying to protect us. Since our ego is never going to disappear, fear-lingering and repeating patterns will continue. So I think it is important to have ways to deal with fear.

It is really important to be aware enough to know what is playing in the background that is causing us fear. I try my best to not operate from a place of fear but I do have a few that pop up from time to time. To give you an example of recognizing fear, I decided to share three things I've struggled with and what I did to manage these fears. These are the monsters I've created, and I am learning to manage them.

What I Did Before

The first three or four years after my marriage I messed around a lot during my grieving process and I wasted a lot of money and made some bad financial choices. What complicated the situation was that I shifted from doing web contractor work for a large corporation which provided me a steady income to starting a business with very unpredictable cash flow.

About a year after my divorce, I got into a very serious relationship which really took my mind off business. I was having a little too much fun with this new romantic partner and I was not working very hard. I really burned through money since I didn't have much new income coming in. I blew through most of my savings and racked up pretty serious credit card debt. As a result of this, I developed the fear of running out of money. Like a lot of fears, this can paralyze you. I stayed in a place of fear for three to four years if not longer. At the time, I would say to myself, "Don't run out of money...Don't run out of money..." As I mentioned earlier, the unconscious mind doesn't process the negative, so on that level, all it was hearing was "Run out of money... Run out of money..." and I did a pretty good job at obliging. I was also kind of mad at myself because I *knew* better than to think this way.

What I Do Now

What was the remedy? One day I was driving to my mom's, and I was just getting to the top of her big ass hill, when the "Don't run out of money…" tape started playing in my head. Just as I pulled up to her house, I screamed at myself "Stop *fucking* doing this to yourself! This is ridiculous.!" I realized I needed to rephrase what I was saying to myself. I replaced "Don't run out of money…" with "Money is flowing into my life…"

I knew it was all in the language I was using and the subtle energy behind the words. I *had* to replace the messed-up disempowering self-talk I was using. At that moment I finally got real and figured out money doesn't just run out. We have bills and money coming out of our bank account, and we can definitely live beyond our means and make bad decisions, but the only way we *run out* of money is when we stop working. I realized that if I kept working and providing value to people, and if I had the courage to charge what I was worth, I would not run out of money. Even when money was being spent, there would be new money coming in to replace it. This is about understanding flow and even non-linear thinking. The solution was a change in my self-talk, a shift in my perspective, and having the faith to know I would succeed.

My bank balance definitely dipped below zero on more than a few occasions and in those moments, it was definitely terrifying. So technically I did run out of money.

But I survived.

This forced me to lean into my fear of having no money. I learned that the images that played out in my head often were much worse than what happened in the real world. Ultimately, this changed my feelings around the concept of security.

Conventional wisdom implies having a great job and a bunch of money in the bank will give us security. I agree with this for the most part, but we all know *downsizing* happens and we can lose our ideal job and be forced to live on savings. In the back of our heads, a lot of us still feel insecure about our finances even when we have a job. But security comes from a mindset where you know you'll be safe no matter what.

Therefore, the new definition I created for security was that if I have employable skills then I have security. If someone needs what I offer, I can generate an income for myself whether I'm self-employed or work in a corporate environment. My commitment to doing a job well and my ability to solve problems and deliver value will always be in demand. My new belief is that by having skills and the willingness to work, I can create security in any situation.

What I Did Before

My second recurring fear has to do with figuring stuff out for my customers. I've been doing marketing all of my career and providing all sorts of creative services. Technology changes pretty rapidly in my industry. There are a variety of software programs I use, and I must shift gears depending on the project. Sometimes I'm editing videos, other times I'm designing graphics or building a website. All these production tools have different features, and then there are also marketing automation and social media tools. I hop around from technology to technology depending on what project I'm working on.

Sometimes a fear pops up when I'm rusty on a certain tool and I begin to worry I may not be able to figure out how to produce what I promised a client. This usually causes me to procrastinate. One day it occurred to me this was just like background noise and again was a ridiculous monster in my head playing tricks on me.

What I Do Now

The remedy was reminding myself I've been in these types of situations literally hundreds of times. I always figure out what I need, and the customer always ends up happy. This was a big breakthrough for me and has helped me gain focus and have less anxiety. I also have learned to be more confident in the quality of work I'm producing for my clients. The biggest antidote to this fear is to take action. No matter how small the step is towards our target, it gets the energy unstuck.

What I Did Before

This third fear is related to love. I've been divorced for eight years now. Over this period, I've had a few false starts in the new romance department. As I mentioned, one of my more serious post-marriage relationships lasted three years, and I thought she was my forever person. Even though it was pretty amazing, I did walk away from the relationship because I found myself being triggered way too often. What has happened more recently is I worry from time to time about if I'm ever going to meet my true forever love. I spend a ton of time alone and for the most part, I'm fine. But it does get lonely from time to time.

What I Do Now

What was the remedy? I basically got real and thought to myself "What if I literally ended up by myself?" I realized I had to be okay with the possibility of this happening. I'd survive if it did and I could learn to love my life regardless of if there was a romantic partner or not. Once I realized there was a distinct possibility that I could end up all by myself and accepted this, the stranglehold of worry over if I'd find someone began to loosen its grip. I go into this more in the *Lover* section later in this book.

I've been talking to friends about what I call "crossing the fear chasm." What I mean by this is that there are times when I feel like I've conquered a recurring fear, but then something happens and I fall back into the old belief pattern. It's like there's this abyss and I get on the other side of it (the safe side) but then there is this magnetic pull that forces me to end up back on the scary side. I then have an "aha" moment and realize that I'm the one *choosing* to live in a place of fear. Once I became aware of this, I was better equipped to face these fears when they arose.

What I found was that I really had to *live through* my most feared situations. I got to see how I showed up in the real world versus the terrifying imaginary scenarios I was making up in my head. I always came out unscathed in the real world. This was a pretty incredible breakthrough and really has helped me feel more impervious and I've been able to put more of a gap between me and the fear chasm. In a way it's like fear is a mechanism that helps us expand and grow.

Warrior Distortion Number Two—Being Overly Aggressive

The other distortion of courage is when someone is overly aggressive. This person must win at all costs and doesn't always play fair. This person always has to one-up you or put you down so they can look good. Let's just say he has a really big and out-of-control ego. In the surfing world, this is the jerk who is always trying to out-paddle everyone and blocks people from grabbing the perfect wake.

Guys are naturally competitive. It's in our blood. We have testosterone for a reason. This biochemistry is in us to ensure our species survives. The world tells us only the strong will survive. As Axl Rose would say, "Welcome to the Jungle."

I have had some guy friends over the years who have had an overly competitive sense about them. These guys always thought they could get all the girls when we went out, and they were always positioning to see who was gonna be the alpha male. There was always a little bravado going on with these guys.

This used to bug me but I just laugh at it now.

What I Did Before

Throughout my adult life, I've had this little voice in my head that said "If I become powerful, I don't want to turn into a jerk." Many people have told me, "Dave you need to take back your power," and "You're too giving," and "You let people walk all over you."

I asked myself recently, "Did the effects of me being abused as a child impact my perspectives around power?" I then realized that on some deep level in the past I felt like I needed to avoid becoming powerful so I wouldn't turn into someone who would overpower people like some of the examples I perceived throughout my life.

I then asked, "Can the issues I have with being overpowered be overcome, and can the hurts from my past totally be purged?" My distorted belief was that power seems in somehow have an element of force and that there needed to be some form of toughness required to get what you need. The logic behind this distorted view around power implies people with power can abuse it and hurt others (me included). And since I've always wanted to be a peaceful person, I've tended to be the subservient person.

That's okay to a degree, but it's not healthy to always be this way.

What I Do Now

As I've evolved, I have a new understanding regarding what strength is all about and how the first step to being worthy is to understand I am connected to God.

Just this connection alone means I have an inalienable right to be treated well by others. When I remember this perception, it gives me the fortitude I need in any situation. The result of this insight, for me, is a foundation and language on how I want to conduct myself. I can stay humble yet know how I want people to treat me. I've cultivated a real sense of presence now and can step into it when I'm around groups and when I do presentations. I've never been afraid to talk in front of people, but I now feel more in command and worthy of respect. Some people may call this taking back my power. I call this remembering who I am and where I came from.

Now when I feel people are projecting on me or acting in a way that isn't appropriate, I strive to be graceful and not have abrupt and forceful reactions. This calm, yet strong response applies to anyone I interact with. For instance, I had a client recently who kept dragging their feet on paying me for website hosting. I realized they were taking for granted the value I provided their company. I decided to tell them I was shutting down their website if they didn't pay by the end of the week. I was polite yet firm at the same time. I've told myself if I'm going to build an enterprise it is important to know how to properly handle infringements in the future. The main idea is to handle these situations with fairness, to have a plan, and to be consistent.

Being concise with our demands and using descriptive words is important because people will know where you stand. As we develop and evolve, the language we use becomes more clear.

Another example of having strength happens In business via successful relationships and ventures, I believe collaboration yields the best work and I enjoy being able to work with other creative people. Collaboration requires a certain degree of competence by each member of the group in order for it to yield optimal outcomes. I really like working with a group of people who are *all* coming from a position of strength. It is more authentic if no one is afraid to say what is on their mind and everyone knows where each person stands. There isn't any manipulation, hidden agendas, or games being played. There is this nice blend of action and respect which really works well.

A great example of unspoken power and presence was personified by the Samoans I went to college with. There were four of these guys of Polynesian descent who were totally badass. They were on the football team and they had each other's back. No one screwed with them because they were a unit. You messed with one, you messed with all of them. And, well, they were *huge* too! For whatever reason, I was on their good side. One night they were at our party barn and some drunk was getting in my face and it looked like we were going to fight when the guy suddenly backed down. I looked behind me and there was Rocket and Matu. They did not say a word, but I have a feeling they gave that drunk a *don't mess with him* kind of look. After this episode, it was nice to know I was on the good side of the Samoans.

The bottom line is this: you can have strength and know you can kick butt if you have to, but your presence is what the other person feels and therefore you don't have to be overly aggressive or try to prove anything to anyone. It's important to realize the subtle difference between being confident and arrogant. There's more on this idea in the next chapter, which is about *integrity.*

Rider Reminders

- Rage can be used in a positive way. Once we are fed up with something like our weight, income, relationships, or whatever, rage provides the spark to get started on a new routine or directive.
- We live in a world full of fear, and it's useful to begin to understand what we fear and to see patterns that repeat themselves.
- If you remember that you've overcome challenging situations in the past, the intensity of fear begins to dissipate.

Chapter Six—Rome Wasn't Built in a Day

"The greatness of a man is not in how much wealth he acquires, but in his integrity and his ability to affect those around him positively." —Bob Marley [9]

Warrior Ideal Number Two—Integrity

Integrity reminds me of a quote by George Zalucki who said: "Commitment is doing what you said you would, long after the mood you said it in has left you."

Keeping our commitments is at the heart of integrity and George's advice is great, but I think people don't understand where integrity truly comes from. It is more than just trying to be a nice guy and having good intentions. You know the saying "The road to hell is paved with good intentions." We want to please everyone we encounter, but that's not realistic. We may have a moral compass, but we need to produce outcomes if we tell someone we are going to do something.

All my life I've wanted to be likable, trusted, and to be a good guy. I've wanted to have morals and ethics, and for the most part, I've lived this way. I always strive to be honest. In some situations, even though those characteristics are wonderful, they weren't really enough. I've known countless people who try hard to be a good person and make a lot of promises so they can please others only to not keep their commitments.

People have forgotten where the meaning of certain words has come from and the word integrity is a prime example of this. I believe at its root integrity is about integrating. It literally means to complete something. This gets overlooked because people are caught up on it being solely a moral issue. My perspectives on integrity are more from a structural viewpoint versus coming from a judging moralistic perspective. Working with materials and processes you have in your life is what helps you deliver on your promises and therefore this is what causes you to have integrity.

For several years I've preached to clients about how important it is to have both structure and creativity. They go hand in hand. For instance, say you are an amazing artist, and you have the ability to create pure beauty. Lack of structure might look like not having the proper environment to paint in or the organizational skills needed to keep supplies on hand, which hinders your ability to create. And once you create all those paintings, what are you going to do next? If you don't have the ability to show your work at a gallery, or you don't have an agent to represent you, or the skills to put them on a website, no one is going to see your work or purchase it. This lack of structure hinders the creative process.

I believe integrity is about this marriage of creativity and structure.

Creativity involves asking questions, listening for answers, and then designing and engineering a solution to a problem. It's about making something new, which until that moment, didn't exist in the physical world. Having the ability to be still and to allow new ideas to flow into one's consciousness is a very special talent creative people have, and when this ability is coupled with structure and the ability to execute solutions, it's a great example of how you can foster integrity.

If you look at integrity from a construction perspective, you'll notice there are three integral components. The first piece is figuring what you want to create and then developing a plan to create it. Understanding the time commitment required to deliver the creation is part of this, too—Rome wasn't built in a day! Remember all great things take time to produce and it is important to account for the time it takes to manufacture results. The next piece is the quality of material used and the skills needed to deliver a satisfying result. The last piece is the follow-through, the action required to finish the task you promised to complete.

I had an episode with a client a couple years ago who questioned my integrity because a project we had been working on for three years had not gotten the results we wanted. He was rightly full of doubts due to an assortment of things that happened during our engagement. Some of the issues were on him because he changed the scope of the project, and was not always available. But, honestly, some issues were my fault, too.

When he questioned my integrity I was pretty upset because I didn't see myself being in the wrong, and the lack of results we had was due to other people.

His accusations stung at first, and I couldn't put my finger on what it was I was feeling. I felt angry and insulted because my character was in question. I felt hurt, threatened, and undervalued. I felt like my morals were being doubted. After a while, I realized I couldn't operate in this emotional state anymore, and so I really dove into some self-evaluation and discovered he was right. I did indeed have integrity issues, and then I realized this affected all areas in my life.

When this issue of lack of integrity finally came to the surface, I figured out then that on an unconscious level I had a need to keep things very gray with most of my clients. It became clear to me that I needed to employ more precise language along with detailed agreements.

I understand now I had a need to keep things gray out of a deep-seated fear I had that I would disappoint the customer by not doing a good enough job. At the time I had issues with boundaries in my personal life, and this was spilling over into the relationships I had with my customers. I decided to dive into the topic of integrity and learn as much as I could, and I discovered integrity goes much deeper than just being honest and keeping your word.

When you look up the definition of integrity, the dictionary states, "1. A sound, unimpaired, or perfect condition. 2. The state of being whole, entire or undiminished."

It's also, fun to look at the words similar to integrity such as "integral" "integrate" and "integer"

The word integer in Latin means "whole."

So yeah, no matter how you slice it, the words integer, integral, integrate and integrity are a big part of a whole dude. You want to be whole and you want the people you make agreements with to be whole too. If you commit to someone but don't deliver on your promises, you are leaving the other person not whole. On the flip side of this, if you are letting people in your life take advantage of you then you are the one not whole.

Integrity reminds me that there are no shortcuts to get from point A to point B. You have to have a plan and take all the steps.

If you think about it, we are literally constructing our life. The caliber of materials used, our daily plan, and the execution, all work together. Each is an integral component that affects the quality of our life. When we truly understand this idea, we can live all aspects of our life with integrity. If any one of those pieces is missing, we are out of integrity with ourselves.

Part of being in integrity with yourself is related to how well you take care of your health. I compare wellness to a wheel with six spokes: physical, mental, emotional, spiritual, relational, and environmental. If one of these spokes is missing or weak that wheel isn't going to roll very well.

In order for the Warrior to have the strength necessary for success, he needs to have all six of the spokes of the wheel accounted for and included in his routines.

Physical wellness is a big part of being a Warrior because it helps us have the strength needed to achieve our goals. It's important to know what you are putting into your body. Understand that what you eat, the supplements you take and therapies you use, all affect how well you optimize your physical body. Taking time to exercise is vital. The amount and quality of water you drink is also important to physical fitness. Water is a big part of our life and it's estimated that our bodies consist of 70–80% water.

The Warrior's environment is often overlooked. Our body is bombarded by microwave oven radiation, and electromagnetic frequency radiation from phones, Wi-Fi routers, and cell towers. How cluttered and messy our home is can also affect this environmental energy.

I go into a lot of detail regarding relational and spiritual attributes of a whole dude later in the book, but I'd like to briefly discuss mental and emotional wellness.

A lot of people lump emotional wellness in with mental health but I think they are two very different topics. Depression and a bunch of different disorders certainly have to do with biochemistry but they're not all related to our brain. There is a ton of research related to how various emotions affect our organ gland system and hormones. In the Extras section of the book I talk more about these studies related to our emotions.

Mental wellness in my opinion has more to do with our brain health and when it is declining our abilities decrease. This may include being forgetful, having difficulty with focusing on a task or problem solving. As you can see this is very different from emotional problems.

Being whole is when all of these spokes are working together in a way that helps you build strength. Grit, determination and fortitude are all words to describe a warrior. I think everyone can get their head around this, but how do you build those qualities? In my opinion this is about picking a target and taking steps toward it continuously. This requires the mental and emotional capacity to measure and manage your results. Many people, including myself, struggle with commitment and accountability..

I was wondering why people resist the concept of being accountable. It's one of those words that feels like you're being sized up and there seems to be some judgment around it. I did my little deconstruction trick and broke the word in half and flipped the order. It went from *accountability* to *ability a count*... or the ability to count.

That doesn't sound too bad now, does it? It doesn't feel like you're going to be shamed for not doing your part. It's just saying you have the ability to count.

Here's another trick that helped me. If you know yourself well enough, you know what drives you and helps you stick to your goal. With this knowledge of yourself, you can create your own personalized system of accountability.

When I struggle to lock in new habits, I occasionally work with a very simple scorecard to help measure activities I want to incorporate. It's a list of items I track on a form each day and then total everything up at the end of the week. I don't really get too caught up on what my score is because it really is about just having the desire to hold myself accountable—you can't manage what you don't measure, right?

One item typically on my scorecard is to get three things done each day. When I achieve those three items, I feel like the day was a success, and I receive the confirmation that I'm going in the right direction and living in integrity.

The interesting thing about to-do lists is the feeling we get when we finish something on the list. When we check the *done* box, there's an endorphin release. The little dopamine hit we get by checking off a task is our biological reward for keeping a promise with ourselves. When we finish something on our list, we're taking one more step toward completion, and being honest with ourselves.

Something related to integrity is the subject of ethics. At the core of ethics is the type of exchanges taking place between people. Let's face it, some people are all about taking and some people are all about giving. If the parties involved are all equally exchanging then everyone is being ethical because each person is whole. .This is about agreeing on what value each person brings to a situation, and this applies to any relationship. In business, it's as simple as what a vendor is going to do for a customer while charging a fair price for a product or service. An example of an exchange being unethical would be when a vendor charges too much and is cheating the client. Another scenario may be when a vendor cuts his price and therefore has to skimp on materials or effort and does not produce a good enough outcome.

The other side of the equation is when the customer is too demanding or doesn't communicate his needs well enough or doesn't pay enough. I've struggled with this for a long time —I've often undervalued my work and undercharged customers, and then it keeps me stuck on a hamster wheel of economic desperation, or mediocrity at best. The key for me lately has been to understand the value I deliver to my clients and being sure that each of us feel whole in our transactions through equal exchanges.

Warrior Distortion Number Three—Low Standards

How do *you* personally define not being in integrity?

We think it's easy to identify people out of integrity and we often judge them. We get this uneasy feeling and we question if we can trust someone and second guess everything they say and do.

However, as a species, we can only recognize something in others if we can recognize it in ourselves. Lately, I've felt that whenever I'm feeling triggered by someone else's supposed lack of integrity, it is God telling me I need to check my integrity as well. How solid am I? How often do I follow through on what I say I'm going to do? How good is the quality of my work? What outcomes am I generating? Am I sticking to a plan? How is my health?

What I'm trying to do here is remove the idea that integrity is only about morals. I'm focusing on being real and looking for ways to improve in a practical sense. I'll be as bold as to say we all have bouts with having a lack of integrity. The only time you would be immune to a lack of integrity would be if you just did nothing.

What matters most is striving to live in integrity with ourselves and this happens as a byproduct of our habits and the quality of life we choose to live.

One of the extremes related to being out of integrity has to do with having low standards. Remember how I described integrity as having three components—excellent materials, a great plan, and good implementation? If you're in a situation where any or all of those are missing and you still accept your results, then your standards are too low.

It doesn't make you a bad person. We all have free will and we choose what we feel is acceptable. Integrity has to do with our choices. If you are consistently letting things slide or just coasting along with little action or structure in your life, then you probably have low standards. I'm starting to think there's a correlation between low standards and low self-esteem. This applies in your personal relationships, and it most certainly shows up in your career—if you don't really think your work is valuable, you're going to struggle in your career whether you have a job working for someone else or if you're self-employed. In either scenario, business or relationships (we'll dive deep into personal relationships and standards in the Lover section), low standards relate to your esteem and how much you value yourself and your abilities.

This is about the caliber of the outcomes you're willing to accept and how much effort you are willing to put in to complete tasks..

Don't confuse what I'm saying here about low standards as being judgmental or thinking one person is better than another because they have higher standards. This is about *energy*. Everything has a way of repeating itself and like attracts like. My Dad used to say to me when I did my chores "Don't do that half-assed." What he knew was that the way you do one thing is the way you will do everything, and if I formed sloppy habits as a young person, chances are those patterns would continue to repeat the rest of my life. (Thanks, Dad!)

There is an energy to something being clean, engineered well, thoroughly prepared, and mindfully created. This energy feels good to be around. I call this *coherent energy*. On the other hand, there is a subtle energy around things that are filthy, disorganized, and done *half-assed*. This energy has an anxious feeling and doesn't feel as good as the pristine scenario. This is a distorted or incoherent energy.

I don't really care what you decide to settle for, I really don't. I just want you to be aware that you are the one choosing what is acceptable to you. This has nothing to do with one person being better than the other, it is only about the choices we make and the cascading effect they have on each other which result in the circumstances we are in right now. The hazard of your choices is that their caliber tends to repeat over and over.

In business, if the quality of your work is low you aren't going to be able to charge a lot of money for what you do and you'll keep attracting low-paying customers. Eventually, you have to make a time commitment and put forth the effort to improve your skills. If not, you will always struggle. If you invest in yourself and seek out training or coaching, you can figure out at what current level your skills are and put together a plan to refine what you do and get better. Here's a pro tip: if you are going to invest in yourself, pick the thing you love doing the most—pick something that gets you excited to get out of bed in the morning.

Also, we have to believe in ourselves and know we can improve. When we have low self-worth, we doubt ourselves too much to make any changes. It is a vicious cycle of not believing in yourself and then not improving. It's important to take a leap of faith in whatever it is you do and take a chance and embrace change. You can eventually get the training or experience you need to improve over time if you commit. But it definitely starts with belief in yourself. Eventually you'll be able to build your skill and core strength and you'll be able to ride that wake like a pro.

What I Did Before

One thing that affects my integrity relates to the length of time it takes for me to finish projects. Either I'm unrealistic in my estimates on how much time really goes into doing something or the other issue may be that I get too distracted and bounce around between too many things. Some people accuse me of being ADHD and they may be right. I see it as an advantage, but I do know I could use more structure in my life. One blessing of this supposed ADHD is the ability I have to envision the big picture and also see all the little details required to get something done.

What I Do Now

The main thing I'm starting to get better at is paying attention to time and not waiting until the last minute to get things done.. When I work on a project for a client, I write down the time I start and finish and bill accordingly. I also feel like my standards previously were based on just surviving. A mindset of poverty and scarcity can be difficult to break out of.

But it can be done.

First, become aware of what you're settling for, Then take baby steps towards improving your circumstances. This may look like making a small increase in your price or scheduling time in your day for continued education. You can have higher standards one decision at a time. The trick is to *stay focused* on what is in front of you at each moment.

In my estimation, people don't go out of their way to have a lack of integrity. Instead, it's the result of each individual choice we make day after day after day to form our habits, behaviors, and beliefs. This creates our reality.

Some people just accept their circumstances and don't realize there is something beyond their current reality. Habits can either dig us into a rut or propel us forward into living the life of our dreams. If we can become aware of our lack of integrity and our leaks, we can make a shift and gradually improve our lives and love the reality we create.

Warrior Distortion Number Four—Arrogance

The other extreme of being out of integrity in my opinion is arrogance. You can have fear or incompetence and hide it through arrogance. How does this relate to integrity? I think people use arrogance as a tool to manipulate people and hide the truth.

Incompetence, arrogance, and integrity all play a little game together. It's a game of deceit. Sort of like a shell game where you shuffle things around and cause the other person to take their eye off the little ball.

In the case of arrogance, the behavior is more subtle and happens when the person believes they can get away with something. One way this happens is with the *fake it til you make it* attitude. This is where the person thinks they know just a little bit more than the next guy. It's like a game of pretend where the person thinks they can produce results, but not really sure how they will get them, yet would never admit this to the other person.

This happens when people say things like, "Oh yeah I got this" and "This is great and is going to be easy." I hate to admit it, but when I hear people say stuff like this to me, a tiny little red flag goes off in my skeptical little mind.

There's a big difference between being fake and arrogant versus having confidence because you've done a task many times before. Confidence comes when it truly is easy for you, and you have great skills in a particular area. Arrogance, though, is a trick people play to mask their lack of skill or hide a concern they have. Someone who comes across as being cocky is probably being this way out of fear and is probably not coming from a place of integrity. People have caught on to this and now say to "either put up or shut up."

If you're really good at something, try not to let your pride get out of hand. Being boastful is also seen as being arrogant. You don't want to rub people the wrong way. There is always someone just waiting for you to mess up, and they're going to want to come and kick the chair out from underneath you and knock you down a few notches. As a culture, we love to see the underdog raise up and dethrone the champion.

We've seen this with the rise and fall of countless leaders.Having a superiority complex in any form is a disaster waiting to happen. The reason I say this is because if you are up in your head all of the time being arrogant, chances are you are going to take your eye off the ball and make mistakes or fail at completing the task at hand.

I've been around a few arrogant people who got blindsided and even had their careers ruined. There's a lot to be said about staying humble because we are never finished learning. There are always ways to improve and new ideas and perspectives if we open ourselves up to study and continue to learn. We are always expanding, and new teachers and opportunities to grow seem to always pop up in our life.

Being too arrogant to learn is being out of integrity because we deny opportunities to improve. Ideally we can have the balance of humility and willingness to learn no matter what and do our best job when we take on a task. When someone is arrogant, results are replaced with drama and excuses.

Integrity is like the glue holding together The Whole Dude puzzle because it leads to the next phase of the Warrior development. He can deliver on what he says he's going to do because he has practiced at his trade. He's seen everything because he's done his work. He not only has the plan and skills to deliver results, but also experience under his belt—he knows how to react even in surprising situations.

This leads us to our next Warrior ideal: Grace under pressure.

Rider Reminders

- Integrity is beyond morals and honesty
- Knowing what causes integrity is important versus just making a snap judgment about someone
- Integrity is the result of having a great plan, using the best materials and talents available, great communication, and follow-through
- Integrity results from the blending of creativity, structure, and execution

Chapter Seven—Your Strength is in the Pause

"The true strength of a man is in calmness."
—Leo Tolstoy [10]

Warrior Ideal Number Three—Grace Under Pressure

It's one thing to be calm when everything is smooth and copacetic. A mature Warrior knows how to be calm in the heat of battle or during a big storm. His quiet confidence comes from knowing all will work out because he put in the practice.

The Warrior Wake Rider knows how to stay sturdy and strong as the sea tries to buck him off his board.

I picked Grace Under Pressure as an ideal because it starts to expand the Warrior beyond courage and discipline. This chapter illustrates the Warrior's ability of producing results when the pressure is on and he's handling tough situations in the moment they occur.

Learning skills, training, and committing to finishing your work, are a big part of being a Warrior. The payoff of consistent practice is that you can perform under pressure because it's like you've built this *muscle* that springs into action in tough situations. If you grasp this concept, it can change your view on having to practice.

The way to achieve under pressure happens by remaining present and pausing as intense situations arise. Animals are not wired this way. When animals have a stimulus happen to them, they have an immediate response, and they have to rely solely on their reflexes. What differentiates Man is his ability to pause before his response.

During the pause you can observe a situation clearly as it develops and don't need to have a knee jerk reaction. In that moment you are collapsing time and you are tapping into true infinite potential. You are merging your gut feelings with the infinite wisdom your heart has access to.

The Whole Dude

Some people seem to be built for those high-pressure situations and it is like watching magic when they perform. A very memorable example of this is David Freese's epic clutch performance in the 2011 World Series. By the way, he went to the same high school as I did, so Freese is a particular favorite of mine. He had a great Series just by the fact that his batting average was over .520. The real magic happened during game six which was an elimination game. The Cardinals had to win, or their memorable season would be over.

The lead see-sawed back and forth between the Cardinals and Rangers. In the eighth inning the Cardinals were down by two runs when Freese came to bat. Even though the Rangers were in a no-doubles defense, Freese was able to hit an opposite field double off the right field wall which scored two runs to tie the game. After that it seemed like anything was possible.

The Cardinals lost the lead in the 10th inning and it appeared the season was going to end. But then what seemed like a miracle, happened AGAIN. With two outs and a 3-2 count, Freese hit a three-run homer for the win and ensured a game seven. And the crowd went crazy.

Those moments will forever be legendary to the fans of the St. Louis Cardinals. It is like time stood still and that moment is frozen into baseball lore forever. I can still picture the look on David's face as he slammed his helmet on the ground between his legs as he was coming down the third baseline seconds before being mobbed by his teammates as he neared home plate.

Seeing epic moments like the Freese three run homer in extra innings reminds us of what *we* are all capable of when we breathe and pause and connect our head, gut, and heart in these do or die situations.

Not to diminish this feat in any way, but I imagine David Freese probably visualized this situation thousands of times and even practiced the scenario over and over again as an athlete. When this once in a lifetime opportunity presented itself he was in the zone where he didn't even have to think and he just sprung into action. My guess is that it was largely a matter of his muscle memory reacting to the stimulus. And—

Holy cow!—I'm pretty sure Freese partied like a rock star that night.

There is a lot of bad mojo in the world right now because no one seems to take a pause before leaping into action. Everyone needs to be blunt and speaks without a filter. While it is definitely important for a Warrior to stand up for his beliefs and speak his truth, a mature Warrior does this with grace because he pauses and has sense and sensibilities.

Everyone's attention span is short because we are all in a hurry to get somewhere or get something done. As a result, anyone who is trying to be influential is trying too hard to be raw and speak their *truth* to capture and keep people's attention. My point here is there is a subtle energy that underlies the rawness which shows there is no pause sometimes.

I think being able to stay calm is a beautiful thing during this crazy time where so many people are overly aggressive. When you control your emotions, your calm energy helps other people get control of theirs. It takes practice to get good at this. Calmness results from being very still, pausing, and detaching slightly from the situation.

This reminds me of how the Buddha is calm whether he's sitting on the mountain top or in the middle of rush hour traffic. (This is one of the reasons I am glad I work from home most of the time.)

Being in tough situations and experiencing stress is common in our lives but having the ability to gracefully navigate life is a great way of being. Through staying calm, the Warrior knows the best course of action. He can drop down to his heart and assess his emotions and the circumstance at hand to make the decision to either act or not act. To walk away or go to battle, to do nothing or negotiate a diplomatic solution. Even if the Warrior is forced into battle, his biggest strength is to stay calm and keep his wits about him. Like Coach Taylor in *Friday Night Lights* says, "Clear eyes, full heart, can't lose."

Warrior Distortion Number Five—Anxiety

I'm choosing to write about anxiety because it is related to out-of-control emotions caused by anticipating undesirable outcomes. Our ego can take over and play out a lot of potential scenarios which can be fear-inducing and makes us uneasy. I have done a little research into the topic of anxiety for a client of mine who works in the mental health industry.

I wrote articles for them to use in their social media campaigns. The name of this business is Mental Wellness Unleashed. They are truly on a mission to remove the stigma around mental and emotional illness—something very much needed in our world. One article I wrote had to do with the six most common anxiety disorders. It is important to be able to tell if something is situational anxiety or if it is an ongoing disorder. These include:

- Post-Traumatic Stress Disorder (PTSD)
- Obsessive-Compulsive Disorder (OCD)
- Social Phobias
- Specific Phobias due to trauma
- Panic Disorder
- General Anxiety Disorder (GAD)

These disorders are very real and it's helpful to educate people about them to create awareness while not minimizing these situations.

From the outside looking in, the person who is suffering from anxiety may not show any symptoms, and the person could outright look calm. The person could be emotionally paralyzed and unable to take action until the pain caused by inaction hurts more than the fear causing them anxiety. Examples of normal situations which cause anxiety but aren't related to a disorder include:

- Being too afraid to ask a friend or relative for a favor or to contribute to something
- Feeling anxious over asking a co-worker or boss for help
- Speaking to a crowd

The problem is when you never resolve your anxiety you may suffer health consequences. The suppression of emotions and lack of awareness can have an effect on our bodies. Many people are so in their heads they don't realize the emotions are being stored up in their bodies. In the Extras section, I have a report the NIH conducted which studied how our organs are affected by emotional issues.

What I Did Before:

I've had anxiety in my life in different ways, whether it was related to work or relationships, there seemed to be noise percolating on the back burner of my mind that at times was so subtle I didn't even know it was there. Sort of like a low-grade temperature that I don't notice but is affecting my capacity.

It usually takes a few things to pile up emotionally before I realize I'm in a downward spiral. I think stress eating is a big example of a self-soothing behavior we do that we aren't even conscious of.

One very specific pattern of anxiety I think I have healed has to do with my business. There are a lot of performance expectations in the type of services I provide. I've never had anything like a panic attack and I usually always manage to keep my cool in front of customers, but there is definitely pressure to produce results. The way anxiety shows up for me usually is in the mornings. I have to be really careful not to get too sucked into what is going on with the world when I first wake up.

There has been a lot of grief, fear, and anxiety going on lately due to COVID-19. It's easy to get drawn into this pervasive fear if I'm not careful. This is what I was referring to in the Son section when I mentioned being careful about what we invite into our life each day.

What I Do Now:

What typically gets me through this anxiety is having more structure. I now set a lot of alarms on my phone to be sure to do things I know are helping my health, like when to take supplements, when to have a protein-rich snack, and when to leave to go on my daily walk. I have an accountability partner that I talk to twice a week and she helps me keep my initiatives on track.

Being in action keeps me out of my head. The nuns at my school used to say, "The idle mind is the devil's workshop." I used to think they were commenting on having sexual thoughts, but now I know they meant even more. I guess I was distracted when they said this because it was usually followed by my friend Rich getting hit across his knuckles and called an idler.

Regarding business, I have to create my own self-imposed deadlines or things take forever to get done. But I have to be careful to be realistic or these deadlines can be anxiety-inducing. It really is a matter of just getting going on a project. In the process of getting engaged and moving, the anxious feelings dissolve.

A really sweet thing is when you can get a handle on your anxiety and reclaim a lot of energy for yourself. All the energy you were unconsciously putting into a particular worry can be diverted and focused to do more relaxing or productive things. I realize that I'm connected to an infinite source which provides all kinds of solutions. As a result, my confidence has improved because I know I am going to do a good job and produce results for my client.

Warrior Distortion Number Six—Agitated

I refer to being in a place of calm as *my shui*. It's a feeling where I chug along, and nothing gets me down or causes me to get unraveled. If I lose my cool and blame someone else I usually say, "Oh man, you un-funged my shui!" The reality is that no one "un-fungs my shui"—I do it to myself. I'm just saying it's good to be in a calm state as often as possible. It's like trying to be more like the Dali Lama, Krishna Das, or Nelson Mandela.

We talked about anxiety and how it is something we do to ourselves out of anticipating something which hasn't happened and most likely won't happen. The way agitation is different from anxiety is that it is usually reactionary, and often there is another person involved. (The person who we think is *un-funging our shui.*) We use this person to place blame. The other way agitation is different from anxiety is that it can escalate to aggressive behavior if we aren't careful.

A good example of agitation is road rage. If someone honks at us, cuts us off, or tailgates us in traffic, we get this instant *aaaarrrggh* feeling and react with the *yeah, yeah, I hear you, asshole* attitude. Our temperature boils as we feel the anger brewing inside us. Ideally, we can be conscious enough to not let these outbursts rattle our cage, but this stuff happens, and we're human. The key is to catch the agitated feelings quick enough, so they don't spiral into out-of-control anger and retaliation. When we act out, it's because we're not taking a pause—we're just reacting with our fight-or-flight instinct.

People are going to honk at us, and we do make mistakes like dropping things or spilling stuff. I don't think there's too much harm in occasionally losing our cool. There is harm when you lose your cool and direct it at someone, even when that someone is yourself. The key thing to remember here is to become mindful of how agitation can spiral out of control and turns into anger. When you're aware of this happening, you can catch it and prevent it from turning into destructive behavior.

What I Did Before:

At the end of my marriage, a lot of this out-of-control agitation was happening with my wife and me. At first, I wasn't aware of it and I knew we were both losing our cool and fighting dirty. Then I became aware of when this was happening with her and I'd say, "Please stop, please don't spiral down."

Sadly, this tactic hardly ever worked.

When people get in a negative downward spiral, they don't realize it and are unaware they can control it. And that out-of-control downward spiral can result in some real bitterness that lasts a long time. Eventually, if she wouldn't back down, I would just blow up, shout, and go a little crazy.

This got her attention and got her to back down every time. It was out of character for me, and I really didn't want to be that way.

What I Do Now:

Now when I get agitated or irritated with people, I pause and think about the situation. I can feel the energy sometimes in arguments. If the situation gets too out-of-control, I just walk away or sometimes ask kindly to have the discussion another time. Often I realize I'm mostly mad at myself and there's something under the surface that is at the root of what is bugging me.

The point here is that we all are human and are going to have frustrating moments of agitation occasionally. But the more aware we are of its existence in our life, the more we can manage our emotions and do less damage to ourselves and others.

It's important to not lash out at other people and *that* is the main takeaway here

Anger is a very real thing and if it spirals out of control, it can be a destructive force. Society tells us to not get angry, to stuff our feelings and take the High Road. But *managing* agitation is what matters, not just ignoring it.

Consequently, anger can be useful and can be leveraged. But it's a balance, too, because you can't go through life being pissed at yourself all the time.

Now when I do something klutzy, I just laugh instead of getting agitated. Those little mistakes are just opportunities for me to laugh. A mistake is a "miss" take and an opportunity to redo stuff.

You get another take.

No big deal.

As long as no one gets injured, then there is no harm really, especially when we can see an opportunity to learn from the mistake.

What I Did Before:

I used to be pretty numb to things going on around me when I was younger because I was often in a place of fear. Being affected by other people's agitation is a real thing and can even create trauma that might need to be dealt with later in life. I felt people's agitation but didn't really understand what was under the surface causing it.

Something that unhinged me when my dad was alive was how angry he could become with other people. He was an intimidating guy at times, and if you merge this with his pessimistic attitude, you can imagine how a lot of agitated situations popped up.

My dad was a big believer in Murphy's Law. If you're not familiar with it, good. But basically, it states if something can go wrong, it will. And as we know, this does actually happen if this is your belief. Negative expectations attract negative things. One example of this working is how irritated Dad would get when shopping—there was more than one occasion when he got so aggravated with someone in a store that he'd just storm out of the place, leaving his shopping cart right there.

Another example is how he reacted to how other people drove. I have to laugh now at some of the things that came out of his mouth. A few of my favorites now include "Assholes of the world, unite!" or "Damn Sunday drivers!" There was something about Illinois Drivers that drove him *nuts.* I haven't quite put my finger on it, but it reminds me a little of the psychotic yet comical outbursts of *Seinfeld*'s George Costanza and his dad. Now I just laugh at the memories of how agitated he became because of these little things. But back then, it did rattle me a bit.

What I Do Now

What I do now is to try to learn as often as I can from whatever I'm doing, even in agitating situations. As I reflect on my growth, these experiences were great teachers. Now instead of being volatile in my reactions, I resist the urge to get upset. Instead I remain centered and let the irritation pass through me quickly. If I need to walk away from a situation or do some box breathing, I have a plan now.

I realize now that the other side of the agitation coin is how I'm learning to not be so passive about things, either, because these little irritants cause unease. For instance, I've become very aware of subtle things draining me. I'm calling these energy leaks. These can be mental, emotional, or physical. A few examples include:

- Not getting enough sleep
- Not eating well
- Being distracted by social media
- Paying late fees
- High-interest rate credit cards
- Being caught up in the need for drama
- Not drinking enough clean filtered water
- Exercising inconsistently
- Drinking too much coffee
- Not taking supplements
- Worrying what people think of me or what i do
- The need to quickly reply to a text or phone call

My goal is to be aware of these very real situations and address them without judging myself for allowing them to happen in the first place. More importantly, this is about focus. The more energy escaping me towards these situations and unconscious thoughts, the less energy is available for me to be creative or produce the outcomes I'd like to see happen.

I'm also starting to realize *focus* is currency. What we focus on is what we get. If we focus on fear, more things show up for us to be afraid of. If we focus on being productive and getting our work done, we get more work done (and make more money). If we focus on things happening with ease, life seems to run smoother. Since we are not focusing on all the *assholes of the world uniting,* we're no longer creating barriers. Instead, we're allowing things to naturally flow as they're intended to.

When we slow down and just *breathe,* we not only begin to realize we have the strength to have a clear mind, but we begin to see from other people's perspectives and put ourselves in their shoes.

This is the last stage of development for the Warrior: Diplomacy.

Rider Reminders

- Performing under pressure is the result of practice and experience.
- Confidence can be built by knowing that you've put in the work and have done your job over and over. This gives purpose to your practice.
- Quality of life is related to our willingness to practice, learn, and hone our skills.
- Being able to recognize anxiety and agitation quickly can go a long way toward improving our life.

Chapter Eight—Conflict is a Part of Life

"Let us never negotiate out of fear. But let us never fear to negotiate"

—John F. Kennedy [1]

Warrior Ideal Number Four—Diplomat

Declaring diplomacy as an ideal of a Warrior seems a bit counterintuitive. But as I mentioned earlier, each Wave Rider has an immature version and a mature version. The *win at all cost* Warrior is the immature version. Having the capacity to be diplomatic is a mature Warrior ideal.

When the Warrior learns to be a calm and collected force, and synchronizes his head and heart, he becomes the mature Warrior.

Most people want to have an easy and peaceful existence and it is natural to just avoid conflict. The problem is, conflict is inevitable as long as people have free will and differing opinions.

One way I envision how diplomacy works is to picture two Native American Chiefs whose two tribes are in a very hostile battle and losses are mounting rapidly on both sides. It becomes apparent that enough's enough and the leaders from each side realize they need to step up and create a peaceful resolution that benefits both tribes before each completely devastates the other.

What is the point of victory if both sides lose everything in the process?

Each of these leaders is held in high regard by their tribe and the two leaders can sense this in each other. A mature Warrior can utilize his calm yet commanding presence to develop skills that can be used to resolve conflicts. He has developed his skills and becomes a leader. He has vision because he has seen many scenarios play out. He has experienced many different outcomes. Nothing really shocks him anymore. I think this makes it easier to see that there are many ways that a conflict can be resolved.

How do you become diplomatic? It starts when someone knows both sides of an issue and has asked enough questions to not only have a clear understanding of the situation but also the ability to debate either side of it. The diplomatic Warrior finds common ground and figures out a way to satisfy both parties.

This has shown up for me lately as I tend to be the person who keeps the peace between my oldest daughter and my ex-wife. I try to have empathy for both of them when they're arguing. I act like a referee to make sure they fight fair and aren't too manipulative. I function as a buffer for them and I do my best to not pick sides. If my ex has a good point or sound logic in her argument, I tell her I think it makes sense. If it's a debatable point, I tell her this, too. And if it's insignificant in the grand scheme, I tell her she needs to know how to pick which battles to fight. I do the same with my daughter.

Both make good points and I try to help them each see the other's perspective. What I'm striving to co-create with my ex-wife and daughter is a new framework so they can interact with each other fairly without too much hurt and drama. We're creating a place where each person respects the other and fosters better communication, and prevents tempers from flaring and feelings getting hurt. These rules of engagement are a guidance system to go back to when things get out of whack.

As a divorcee, I could automatically just side with my daughter out of spite from the divorce. But I don't do that because it would do more harm than good. Although it's tempting sometimes, it wouldn't be very good co-parenting and it would be a poor example for my daughters.

Men need skills on how to communicate non-violently and to learn to be a bit more compassionate. It's important to be able to stand your ground when needed, but also to be able to step back from time to time and really consider the other person's point.

What seems to be going on right now in society's *cancel culture* is really sad. Not only are people ending relationships and severing ties, but frankly, they're being too lazy to consider another perspective to operate from.

Being able to see more than one side of things is wise and benefits your long-term health. Being diplomatic is about creating a safe space for people to communicate their differences and to devise strategies to resolve them. It's about being able to realize that conflict is a part of life, but you don't have to always be on the defensive worrying about being attacked by someone.

Diplomacy happens when both people can come to a place of respecting each other. Think about it: if your opponent is willing to go to battle to defend his belief system and is devoted to winning at all cost, there may be something in their message worthy of listening to. If you can just pause and really listen to your opponent (or the mediator), you will begin to see that there is a lesson within this clash of ideas that everyone can learn from.

I feel that we live in an era where people quickly dismiss their opponents' view point and this is often done with limited information. Now more than ever it seems important that everyone learn strategies to resolve conflicts and accept each other. Sadly the old paradigm of using manipulation, gaslighting, fear tactics, guilt-tripping, and shaming is taking its toll on civilization. It is so prevalent it seems that we don't even notice it happening. My hope is that we can learn non-violent solutions that benefit everyone and old behaviors such as bullying and dismissive tactics will be noticed right away and rendered useless by everyone.

Warrior Distortion Number Seven—Avoids Conflict

The passive distortion of the diplomatic ideal is avoiding conflict. Earlier today I was thinking about when I was kind of in a dark and deep place toward the end of my marriage (literally). I was working with a shaman on some energy issues. I'm pretty sure my ex-wife to this day has no idea I was working with a shaman. Like I mentioned earlier, I hid a lot of things like this from her back then. Also, there were some very peculiar things happening to me that seemed rather mystic. Like randomly having priests appear five days in a row (this happened the first time I was considering leaving my wife). I was at a stage when I was beginning to learn about boundaries and shielding myself for the first time. I was spending more time going inward and digging more into some very esoteric topics. My wife sarcastically said, "I was going off the Richter Scale."

I was also in a very spiritual place in my life and I wanted a way to embody the holy feelings I was having. I started learning yoga from a yogini who had previously lived in an ashram. I could tell Sherry (my yoga teacher) was very devoted to living a deeply spiritual lifestyle, and therefore I chose her as a teacher. She lived at the edge of St. Louis City where everyone had detached garages. She renovated hers and turned it into a groovy little yoga studio.

She was a very legitimate yoga instructor. She also performed Vedic fire ceremonies, educated people about Hinduism, and offered a variety of other self-discovery experiences. It was a little precarious for me because I always felt like I was on the fringe of this "woo-woo" stuff. Even though it all resonated with me and I had a lot of profound visions and deeply meaningful experiences, I never really thought I was a legit member of the *vibe tribe* because I still felt a little too *west county-ish*. I didn't feel quite hippy and tree-hugging enough, but then again, I was pretty far out there compared to my suburbanite friends. So, who the heck was I and how the hell did I even come across a shaman? I guess I'll blame it on Facebook.

On one particular night, the Shaman I was working with performed what she called a soul retrieval ceremony with a group of us seekers at Sherry's studio. What I was anticipating was a peaceful, heavenly, and angelic experience, but this is pretty much the opposite of what happened.

At the beginning of the ceremony, the shaman brought us into something like a guided meditation. We laid in a circle all nice and cozy, and she rhythmically beat on her drum and chanted, and hypnotized us into a deep trance-like state.

During our journey, she told us to visualize the entrance of a cave and instructed us to push on part of the earthy outside wall, and a door would open. She said if the passageway wouldn't reveal itself this meant we needed to be purified before we could enter. If this happened, we needed to go down the path to a nearby stream of water and bathe. This would make us worthy of going into this sacred place. My door wouldn't open, so I needed to visit the visualized stream. After my mystical bath, I went back and was then able to enter the cave.

I squeezed through a tight crevice and found a muddy path which eventually led to a very large, cavernous room. It was faintly lit and very earthy-smelling. Just as I entered, I slipped and slid down a hill into a big puddle of mud.

Suddenly out of nowhere, I was attacked by an indigenous person, and I was thrust into a battle that was very physical and violent (even though this all was happening in my mind). I was initially in a state of shock and thought "Where the heck did this dude come from, I'm trying to find my soul... WTF..."

Then it occurred to me to fight back and defend myself. We fought and fought, and it got pretty violent. After a while, I was able to wrestle control and overpower this hostile entity. Just as I was becoming fully engaged, I was lifted in the air by this huge elephant which appeared out of nowhere. He wrapped his massive trunk around me and lifted me up in the air and placed me into an upper room that overlooked the mud pit. This room had a view of the lower level similar to the balcony area of a theater.

The glow of a campfire dimly lit the room with an orange hue. An elder was there, and I asked him what this was all about. Covered head to toe in dirt and dripping in sweat, I mentioned my shock because I was there for a soul retrieval—I didn't know I'd signed up for an ass-whooping. I thought my soul retrieval was going to be about love, blessings, and all these heavenly things I perceived my soul to be all about.

In essence, the teacher said the battle taught me about conflict and how it occurs naturally in our world. He said conflicts arise in all areas of my life. He said, "Understanding conflict can help you discern when you need to protect yourself and to know when it's time to go to battle."

Up until this point in my life, I avoided conflict because of the environment I grew up in during my childhood. As a kid, I often lived in a place of fear, and there was a lot of anxiety over the turmoil caused by always walking on eggshells around my dad. Consequently, at the time of the soul retrieval ceremony, I was avoiding conflict in my marriage. I was often hiding stuff from my wife to avoid arguments and the ensuing feelings of chaos and disappointment.

As I reflect on this, it makes sense how the ceremony was indeed part of a retrieval of my soul. I always felt like I was a peaceful Zen master kind of person and while this is a great way to be, avoiding conflict *altogether* doesn't serve anyone. In some ways, it denies a part of who you are. We all have raw emotions like anger, frustration, and agitation. It's unhealthy to just stuff them away. When we avoid conflict it stunts our growth. This soul retrieval was a big turning point in my life because, afterward, I started to learn about advocating for myself and not always being a pushover.

What I Used to Do

As a child, I did a lot of things physically to avoid conflict such as staying in my room and going into my own little world. I guess the blessing is how during this time I began my deep love of music. It had (and still has) the ability to transform my mood regardless of the situation. Music was a great way to distract me and tune out all the other stuff going on in my home life. I eventually became a self-taught guitar player and to this day my appreciation of music is a big part of who I am.

Avoiding conflict later found its way into my married life. My (now) ex-wife had very high standards on how she wanted our life to look and how she wanted things done. Every weekend I'd have a big, long to-do list, and I would just get after it and never question anything. I did whatever I needed to complete the tasks on the weekend to-do list and went along with this for several years because I did not want to have arguments. I wanted to be a good husband and team player. Eventually, it got to the point where I just said, "Okay Debbie, what is it you want me to do?" and "How do you want this?" I just kind of gave up on how I thought things needed to be, and just acquiesced and let her call all the shots.

I gave up my authority. Some people would call this giving up my power, but in reality, I hardly held onto any power ever in my life, so there wasn't much to give up. Gradually this led to her losing respect for me, and then she accused me of not knowing how to think for myself. Kind of crazy how it evolved.

My friends got a kick out of how I needed to be *productive* every weekend, but it was my way of keeping the peace and justifying my existence. It got to the point where I thought if I wasn't making money, helping with the kids, cooking, or doing something around the house, I was disappointing my wife. The distorted view I had during my married life was a perception that couldn't be sustained. I will admit being in my head a lot and in a victimhood mentality, really caused me to miss out on a lot of potential joy. I was in defense mode so much I wasn't present to what was *really* going on with my family at times.

What I Do Now

I've shifted my belief about why people become confrontational and realize people are processing whatever is going on with their life. Even though people can be harsh, I realize they aren't always necessarily coming from the best versions of themselves and this isn't who they truly are. People are also very committed to their beliefs and are willing to fight for them.

When people attack, it isn't always physical. Sometimes, it's the words they use and the tone they say them in. It can even be the *lack* of words, like a mean stare. Even physical attacks may not be violent, such as when someone tries to intimidate you by getting into your personal space.

I now view facing conflict as a way to develop my discernment skills. It's like a practice in decision making as I navigate these situations. The Warrior has the ability to pause and assess the situation to determine if he should go on the attack, run away, or do nothing at all.

Avoiding conflict 100% of the time is not healthy in the long run because you never really become battle-tested. If you've been coddled all your life or too meek, you won't know how to stick up for yourself. And I pretty much guarantee at some point you're going to face tough challenges.

One last thought about conflict as it relates to diplomacy: really, it's a way to *learn*. Think about it…if you're in a situation where you're facing someone willing to stand up— to fight—for their beliefs and convictions, there may be something you can learn from this foe. Maybe they have an ideology you've never been exposed to. What if your current belief system is flawed? Maybe there's a message in there for you somewhere. I'm not telling you to be a pushover, but consider expanding your emotional capacity to recognize the message and not kill the messenger.

Warrior Distortion Number Eight—Won't Budge

Another character who shows up in diplomatic situations is the person who will not budge in the negotiations. This person is so sure of being right they just can't see the other person's side. During disagreements, this person becomes cemented into their position, so caught up in their own way of thinking that they simply can't envision reality being any other way.

In Susan Cooke Grouders' report *The Nine Stages of Ego Development,* she talks about the Conventional Stage. This phase of development is the level about 70% of the world's population is at. People at this stage of development are very committed to social norms and think everything outside of the norm is weird or evil. They are realists who are very much into their tribe, and their beliefs and biases paint their reality.

Two subcategories at this stage are the Conformist and the Expert. The Conformist sees things very black and white and is basically unaware of the myriad ways a scenario can play out. Things and people are either right or wrong and there is no in-between. They say they just want the facts. These people just go along with what they are told by authority. The slang word to describe these people is *Sheeple.* They're very committed to going with the crowd and doing the *right thing.* It is interesting to watch people like this in an argument because eventually, they run out of *facts and logic* to support their view, and they usually get angry or change the subject. A new word I'm starting to use to describe these folks is *Sleeple.*

According to Grouder, the next evolution is the Expert. This person is educated and has specialty information they've acquired over the years through traditional education. Many are considered subject matter experts and may have even received accolades for their knowledge. They *just know* because of all their studies and experience THEY are right, and YOU are wrong!

In confrontational situations, someone at this level will blatantly ridicule other people to reinforce how right they are, and to prove the other person is an idiot! They will cite references to studies, books, and their own research to prop up their stance on an issue.

As you can imagine, when someone does not have the emotional capacity to wrap their head around an opposing view—let alone see potential benefits of a new way of thinking—creating diplomatic solutions is going to be a problem.

I think the key takeaway here is to stay calm when you are dealing with these people. Remember your strength in the pause and keeping your composure can really do wonders. Your calm demeanor may actually be as important as the points you're making because, eventually, they may sense you aren't insane or evil. Also, accept that you may never be able to come up with an equitable solution when you are in a conflict with someone like this. You may have to pick a different battle and try to be at peace with the outcomes. If this is unacceptable to you, then you may need to find another expert who understands your viewpoint and let that person be the bad guy and argue with the other party.

Understanding differing views and how emotions can spiral out of control and how to navigate these situations are great skills the Warrior can use as he morphs into our next Wake Rider—The Lover.

Rider Reminders

- Diplomatic skills are the bridge to being a more loving person.
- Walking a mile in another's shoes is the root of diplomacy.
- Hold your ground, but be open to hearing a solution that's a win for everyone.
- Don't fear conflict.

Warrior Section Takeaways

The Second B Word—Bearings

It took me a while to decide on the Warrior's B Word.

When I wrote the first version of this book, I figured the B-word should be *balance*. The Warrior has well balanced energy and has a killer instinct, along with compassion. He has the ability to react with cat-like reflexes and also knows the right time to pause and not attack. I thought about the balance between the masculine and feminine energy in all of us and that men don't tend to understand this and felt obligated to talk about this concept. I later deleted most of that content.

The problem I had with using the word balance to remember the Warrior is that it's temporary, I like the concept but I feel we need something more dynamic which accounts for all of the moving parts in life.

The Warrior knows how important it is to push on to finish a task and also knows when to give himself a rest.

The Warrior is all about the fortitude needed to achieve things in life, so *building* seemed like a pretty good word to exemplify the Warrior's essence. I spoke a lot about the construction analogy in the Integrity chapter and how this helps you build your character and it's also very obvious that the Warrior is building strength in order to accomplish his goals.

I then thought about surfing and how you need to have balance to ride a wake, but you have to find the center point and stay with it for a complete ride. This requires practice and the tenacity to build your skills and core strength to handle the force the wake exerts on you.

In the end, I decided a more appropriate B Word for the Warrior is *bearings*.

My Dad used to always say "you have to get your bearings straight" and I never really understood his point fully until just recently. Think about when the surfer makes his transition from laying on his belly waiting on the peak of the wake and then leaping to his feet at just the right moment. Yes, he needs to have a sense of balance to do that, but in reality, he's in sync with the wake. He gets his bearings, holds firm, and rides the wake. He may be wobbly from time to time but he can rely on his strength to stabilize himself. He's invigorated by the ride as he senses the force of the sea as he gracefully rides to shore. Just like the sea, everything in life is in movement. There's a speed, amplitude, and rhythm associated with everything and we can pick up on this when we have our bearings and sync up with life's movement. The Warrior has made the effort and put in the practice to be able to lean into situations and bear down when he needs to.

I decided to dig a little deeper and look up the definition of bearings. It said this:

1. The manner in which one conducts or carries oneself, including posture and gestures: *a man of dignified bearing.*
2. The act, capability, or period of producing or bringing forth: *a tree past bearing.*
3. The act of enduring or capacity to endure.
4. Reference or relation (usually followed by *on*): *It has some bearing on the problem.*

I'm pretty stoked to use this as the B Word for the Warrior because *bearing* truly encompasses everything about the Warrior in one word. This is about our capacity to move forward, to be strong, and have the ability to be a support when called upon. In addition to our initial core rage, we also need our ability to endure, to keep on going, and to see things to completion.

When you are feeling adrift and rudderless in life, remember this B word to help you course correct and get on track. Remember the word bearing and it will remind you of all the ideal Warrior attributes already in you like courage, calmness, diplomacy, and integrity.

Rite of Passage

The Rite of Passage for the Warrior occurs when he goes from victim to victor and realizes something is still missing after he achieves his goal.. It's pretty damn sweet to overcome challenges faced as we set out to achieve our goal. Whether it's the sexy new car, a promotion at work, or landing a big client, the dazzling high of achievement feels hollow if we have no one to share these victories with.

It can be pretty lonely at the top.

This empty feeling is the pain the Warrior still feels after he wins, and is the bridge into the next Wake Rider—the Lover.

Exercise

What is something you want to achieve, big or small? Write it down. Is it a fitness goal? Hold yourself accountable. Start the scorecard process. Seek out the support of a coach, teacher, mentor, or friend. Find a source of inspiration.

PART THREE - The Lover

The Lover Wake Rider
I Won to I One

"May I learn to look at myself with the eyes of understanding and love"

—*Thich Nhat Hanh* [12]

The Lover's Transformation

Love can be very confusing. Feeling desirable to people seems to be a challenge for us. Being confident and *chill* for some reason apparently seems to be a requirement to be attractive to the opposite sex (or at least that's what is depicted in the entertainment world).

Arthur Herbert Fonzarelli did a real number on me as a kid. I was a huge fan of the TV show *Happy Days* and The Fonz was a big influence on me then, and he taught me I had to always be *cool!* I needed to be the kid who was unconventional and rebel against authority. I looked up to him so much I even got into jumping ramps on my bike. If I could have afforded a leather jacket I surely would have worn one.

When I started college, my identity was influenced by the character Nick Cage played in the movie "Valley Girl." He was more brooding and a younger, cooler Fonz. By then, I had spent many years in the water as a competitive swimmer and I always had a nice tan and shiny chlorine bleached blond hair and so I really was able to self-identify with a California Dude persona (even though I lived in Ballwin, Missouri). It seemed like every word out of my mouth was *like, rad, stoked* and *totally awesome*. Was I fake? I don't know…probably.

What I do know is that I was pretty terrified of attractive girls and had to hide behind some sort of Surfer Dude mask. Having said that, to this day, any time I hear those Rickenbacker guitars play the first few notes of "Million Miles Away" by the Plimsouls, I get completely jacked up and they rock me back to the core of who I am no matter what circumstance I find myself in.

So what does pretending to be cool have to do with the Lover? Well, eventually your intimate partner is going to figure you out and people crave authenticity and realness.

Being cool is really about learning to allow things to flow naturally. And when we do, we experience this incredible feeling of wholeness.

The Lover's Desire

The Lover Wake Rider's root desire is ecstasy. This sensation is beyond being happy. Many people have said happiness is a choice.

They're right.

We can certainly pause and decide how we want to react in any situation, and we can choose to be happy no matter what.

Ecstasy, however, is *beyond* happiness.

When we're in a state of ecstasy, we have a major chemical release. We get little dopamine hits all day long by tiny things such as getting a bunch of likes on a social media post or receiving an alert that our favorite stock is up 33%. I can see why people are so addicted to the apps on their phones but these are just little appetizers on the pleasure buffet.

Ecstasy is what happens when everything feels perfect in our life…no worries, no deadlines, no fucks to give—just pure freedom. All you're focusing on is savoring the supreme joy you're experiencing in a solitary moment. We're riding the peak of the wake and we're truly alive.

These moments can come obviously from sex, which explains why our culture can get so obsessed with finding the perfect specimen to be our mate. It's easy to see how people confuse the chemical cocktail released during sex as actual love due to how powerful it feels.

Once we feel ecstasy, we want a big hit of it again and again. This is not just about having a massive orgasm. This could be the result of the roll of the dice or catching an ace on the river or the buzz you get from your third IPA or a hit of really good weed. It could be the feeling you get when your team wins the championship, or eating the perfect meal in a great environment with friends. You can experience ecstasy watching your kids perform well at something they love like music or sports. It can come by finishing a big project or when long-anticipated money finally hits your bank account. It can even come when you're listening to a spiritual teacher sharing an amazing message about love and hope.

Ecstasy is a suspended moment in time that feels like divine bliss. It's there, right at the edge of addiction.

When the Lover gets too attached to ecstasy, compulsive behaviors can result. There's a very powerful drive to experience exquisite things. I'm here to say that if we can ride a wake of ecstasy right to the edge and know how to come back down without crashing, it can add a ton of enjoyment to our life. The God I believe in doesn't have an ounce of a problem with this. The challenge is to stay centered on the wake as we bring the experience to a resolution..

One way ecstasy shows up for me is when my worries evaporate while I'm watching a gorgeous sunset. I feel a connection to this glorious earth and the majestic, colorful sky. I experience a supreme feeling of joy because I have confidence my Creator has my back. During these moments, I feel completely secure and protected and know all is well. I'm not always in this state, but I've experienced it many times and it's a wonderful way of being.

Why This Is Important

I'm convinced that, unless you're a psychopath, you have a primordial urge inside of you that wants to have a connection to people. Whether it's the passion you have for a romantic lover, the kindred spirit you have with a coworker, or the pride you feel when you look upon your amazing children, we all have this foundational drive to connect. And without connections like this in our life, it flat-out *hurts*. I referred to that pain caused by isolation and being alone as the Warrior's Rite of Passage. It's very real. It's important to understand and heal this part of ourselves because many of us are walking around hurt and confused about love.

One reason love is confusing is because we're always learning about ourselves and how things relate to us. Love often seems like a chaotic science project because everyone we're with is really just teaching us about ourselves and mirroring back who we are. And, they're learning about themselves, too, which confounds the situation even more. A lot of us want to find our ultimate forever partner who makes us feel complete. The reality is that *we* complete ourselves. Our mate doesn't complete us.

Our culture romanticizes and distorts the idea of love so much it is like we are in a hypnotic daze 24/7. The message mass media transmits is to focus on what we don't have and to remind us how hurt we are, versus focusing on what we already have and being grateful. This results in a lot of people walking around very confused by the topic of love.

Case in point, as I've been working at the coffee shop on this introduction, the following songs have just played in the background:

"Desire" – performed by U2

"Why Can't This Be Love" – performed by Van Halen

"She's An Easy Lover" – performed by Philip Bailey and Phil Collins

"True Love" – performed by Pink

"Love My Way" – performed by The Psychedelic Furs

"We Don't Have to Take Our Clothes Off" – performed by Ella Eyre

"I've Been Waiting for a Girl Like You" – performed by Foreigner

"What's Love Got to Do With It?" – performed by Tina Turner

"Love is a Battlefield" – performed by Pat Benatar

"Real Love" –performed by Nothing But Thieves

Let's admit that we're very uncertain of what we think people want. We typically think everything is based on the physical world, but it's time to teach men that we are more than just a physical body! Love is more than chasing, conquering, controlling, and *owning* a trophy wife.

I recently did a little impromptu survey on Facebook. I posted this question on my personal page: "Heterosexual women what are 3-5 things you look for in a relationship with a man?" 69 women replied to the post. Some might debate how scientific this is and if the sample size was big enough, but I found the replies pretty interesting. It was informative because the answers varied so much. I tabulated the top 10 most common traits women are looking for. There were about 40 different answers given. I was mildly amused by the top vote-getter which was *humorous*. I think a similar range of answers would occur if men also took this survey.

Love is confusing because we are all unique individuals, and have such wide ranges of experience and biases. If you want to be a great lover, start by acknowledging that your partner is unique and has different perspectives than you. Be willing to accept them exactly as who they are at this moment. This understanding will be a great foundation for any relationship.

Intimate partners need to meet each other where they are and figure out a way to grow together. It is like when you move a plant to a new pot. You want to get one big enough for the plant to continue to grow. Love is like a divine container for the circulation of giving and receiving. The container can be big enough for everything to become beautiful and blossom, or too confining, and the relationship gets suffocated and dies.

Having said all this regarding partnerships, I feel love starts with the relationship you have with yourself. Everyone's circumstance is based on many misperceptions and choices made in the past. No wonder 50% of marriages end in divorce. The point is, we basically have to own all those past choices and still love ourselves. If we choose to have an intimate partner, the same amount of levity and acceptance is due to them too. You need to love yourself first before you can attract your ideal mate.

Relationship coaches talk a lot about creating boundaries and I feel like this is a bit off. This idea implies that we need to be in protection mode. As if you have to protect yourself from being attacked and you need to create a wall or you have to block people out.

That doesn't really feel like loving energy or the willingness to be intimate and vulnerable with a partner. I think a more *whole* strategy is to understand what is important to you and how you want to feel in a relationship. You don't have to stand up to people projecting their issues or manipulating you. This isn't about boundaries. This is about feeling good as often as possible and being able to communicate when it doesn't in a loving way.

This section is not about how well you do in bed with your mate and how well you *perform.* Don't get me wrong, a lot of women do want to have great sex and be desired, and appreciate some eye candy, but sex is only part of the equation. It seems like the focus in today's world is only about physicality and guys sometimes think they need to look like Brad Pitt, Aquaman, or the Rock just to get a girl's attention. There is nothing wrong with those dudes and their appearance and self-confidence is pretty amazing but we are much more than our outside shell. We are multidimensional beings and a dude can connect with women on so many levels, not just the physical.

Who comes to mind when I think of the Lover Wake Rider

There are many examples of the immature Lover depicted on TV and film, but one who jumps out at me is the character played by John Cusack in one of his first films, 1985's *The Sure Thing* directed by Rob Reiner. It portrays many examples of the angst twenty-somethings have when they are trying to figure out love. Cusack's college-aged character struggles to have relationships with girls. He uses trickery and manipulation to try to get girls to be intimate with him and this doesn't work. He's so distraught by his lack of luck with women that he decides to travel across the country to meet a girl his buddy describes as a *sure thing*. Along the way, he inadvertently falls in love with a girl he hitchhiked across the country with, and of course, much drama unfolds between the two of them.

For the mature Lover, a great example that comes to mind is Matthew McConaughey—specifically, how he presents himself in Lincoln auto commercials. He seems to embody this wonderful sense of cool that everyone admires, both men and women. He has this very self-actualized Zen-yet-amorous vibe in these commercials. He single-handedly morphed the stodgy old Lincoln automobile line into a prestigious brand with one commercial where he doesn't even really say anything. He just looked at a bull in the road and said "Whoa." He's taken care of his physical appearance, obviously, but he also has a presence about him. Not only is he confident, but he's also charming, doesn't give off a lot of needy energy, and you can tell he gives people space.

Core Strength of the Lover

The idea of courting (core-ting) is what comes to mind when I think of the strength of the Lover Wake Rider. Men get to experience the phenomenon of pursuing and waiting. The surfer has to paddle vigorously to get out to the wake zone and then has to sit and wait for the perfect wake to surf. He knows he can't control the wake and learns to surrender to this awesome force.

He has figured out the techniques and strategies to successfully ride the wakes. He savors the exquisite nature of riding as he soaks in the ocean spray and witnesses the beauty of all that is.

Becoming a lover is a lot like this in real life. The Lover goes after his romantic partner by putting his heart on his sleeve, and risks getting hurt. He is on his best behavior. His senses are on high alert. He puts his lover on center stage. At the foundation of courting is the Lover's capacity to be aware, attentive, and respectful of the needs of his prospective partner. It's like a dance of going for it and then giving the other person space to be their authentic self. The ability to synchronize with life's rhythm and react gracefully is what's at the core of the Lover—he's surfing the tube, living in the moment, and thankful for everything he already has.

The Sweetness of Life

I truly believe a person's thoughts, perceptions, and beliefs can affect their physical health. In chapter three I alluded to having some challenges related to my health... About ten years ago, I got diagnosed with Type 2 Diabetes. At the time I was very much into holistic wellness and energy medicine, and so I was blown away when I got this news. One of my woo-woo friends recited Louise Hayes who said energetically Type 2 Diabetes has to do with missing out on the sweetness of life. I stewed on this a bit and thought "Well that's pretty fucking vague...thanks, Louise!"

However, I didn't dismiss the information.

I set out to try to understand this *dis-ease* more, especially since this is a huge epidemic not just in America, but the entire world. At first, I thought, "What is the sweetness of life?" From a materialistic standpoint, I had some epic stuff going on in my life at the time. I got to fly in corporate jets. I got to do all the marketing for a multi-million dollar conglomerate. I got to go on amazing trips all over the Caribbean like Little Dix Bay in the British Virgin Islands. I got to stay at the Four Seasons in Wailea and watch celebrities like Dustin Hoffman, Harold Ramis, and Rob Reiner try to fit in with us mere mortals. I had a pretty kick-ass house that I designed and built with a backyard that looked like a resort. From a materialistic perspective, I had a very sweet life.

Then I started to realize my marriage had seemed pretty loveless for the last four or five years, and then I thought, "Well I guess this sweetness has to do with love." I felt certain the disease was triggered by all the hurt feelings I accumulated throughout my life, and I was also feeling like time was slipping through my fingers when I hit my mid-forties.

After I got divorced, I went on a mission to find a deep connection, and I just knew finding true love would heal this disease. I even went so far as to think maybe it was not just the absence of love in my life, but maybe it had to do with my willingness to receive love and how I processed it. When I got serious with my new girlfriend, who I thought was my forever person a year after my divorce, I really focused on how I received love.

What this looked like was a massive amount of sex. I was on a mission to heal and truly felt the path was through sex. It was a lot like Marvin Gaye's song "Sexual Healing" (and maybe it worked some). Regardless, it was amazing and pretty gratifying, to say the least. When it was all said and done the sex really wasn't the answer either, and things seemed to get even worse with my health. I'm sure one of the reasons was because I was triggered all the time in that relationship.

After I moved out and on with my life I kind of forgot about this *missing out on the sweetness of life* stuff for a while and just focused on my work and being a good dad. I decided to get more serious with my physical fitness and got into stuff like fasting, working out more intensely, taking supplements, and eating a low-carb diet. Those lifestyle changes helped to keep my blood sugar in a decent range, but I don't think this healed me.

I spend a ton of time alone, and compared to the average guy I have a lot more opportunities to just slow things down. One by-product of this solo-slow time is how I've really started to notice just how fabulous some things are in life. Like having a relaxing dinner with friends or family. I love being able to hang out with my daughters, listen to what's on their minds, and admire just how beautiful they are on the inside and out.

I cherish the time I spend with my Mom and listening to her talk about when she was a kid riding the trolleys in the city by herself. She tells stories about our ancestors like her Bohemian grandparents and how her grandpa was a tailor who moved to California after his wife died giving birth to my grandfather. During these conversations, it's just super sweet to slow life down and completely collapse time. Then it finally occurred to me:

That....THAT was the sweetness of life I had been missing.

It dawned on me the sweetness of life is about slowing down, paying attention, and savoring as many of these sweet moments as possible. Enjoying and appreciating the time I'm with my loved ones, and not always having to be in a rush, or letting so many people determine how I use my time. It's also about understanding my worth and purpose. It's about how I don't always have to be in a place of fear or lack, worrying about the future. Now I realize this *sweetness of life* comes when I witness how I feel when I'm living from a place of ease versus a place of unease. I can now let the sweetness in.

I let the wake come to me and this is the magic of being alive and the foundation for understanding and experiencing love. By no means is my life easy and I'm not floating in the clouds 24/7, but I'm letting the sweetness in as much as possible now.

That's what the Lover section of this book is all about. In essence the sweetness is about not having to force things and to savor experiences as they melt and unfold.

Chapter Nine—I'm Speechless

"One moment of patience may ward off a great disaster. One moment of impatience may ruin a whole life." —Chinese Proverb

Lover Ideal Number One—Patience

We live in an imperfect world and could potentially go insane by how ridiculous people and situations are at times. But why be miserable? A great antidote to emotional unease is patience—which is why I've started the Lover section with this ideal.

One day, I was scratching my head about what was missing from this section, and my Mom called on the phone. At first, I was in a rush to get off the call because I wanted to get back to writing.

But then I had an "Aha" moment!

When I hung up I said to myself "Oh wow, I have no patience…" and "Man, I need to listen better." Then it reminded me how I need to just relax, chill, and be more present with people and I thought "Wow, this is the missing piece to write about!'

I'm blessed to still have my Mom in my life. I really enjoy downtime with her at her house one or two weekends a month. It's great because I can go there and leave all my worries behind. It's like going on a stay-cation. I overindulge on coffee, home-cooked meals, and relaxation. Everything seems to move in slow motion.

My Mom has a lot of friends and we have a really big family. There is always some current event in her life to talk about. It's good practice for me because it teaches me to just stay still and listen. As much as I want to jump in to change the subject sometimes, I keep my mouth closed and listen to her tell me about all the different people she cares about, and everything going on in their lives. She has a lot of great wisdom to share and I also love bouncing ideas off of her about my life, my philosophies, relationships, and parental issues.

As our Wake Rider progresses along, you can see how his pain and desires relate and how one ideal helps develop the next. When he begins to see others' perspectives and their side of the story this bridges into the Lover's first ideal of being patient and a good communicator.

We all want to be heard and understood. If you're in a hurry or thinking about the next thing you are going to say during conversations, you are not being patient or a good listener. This is a skill we all seem to be needing some help with lately. Whether we are with co-workers, our children, a spouse, or our romantic partner, we can easily forget we are all equal. We forget this person needs to say and do what they want. How we react to what others say to us is very important, and it's another example of being patient: just relaxing and not competing for attention goes a very long way in strengthening our relationships.

Patience also comes into play with communication when people say things we don't necessarily agree with. If we're good listeners, we can pause and not instantly react. If we're mature enough, we can discern and decide if we want to defend our position or if it is better to just not say anything at all. If we disagree with what someone is saying, we can simply ask them to explain why they feel that way. Remember how the Warrior learns about the strength in the pause—this applies here.

Patience is also about allowing people to have space and time to decide what they want. People need time to process their feelings about situations, and it's very important to allow them to get back to you on their time schedule and not have anxiety when they don't get back to you right away. It's about respecting people's time and energy. If you desire to have someone as your intimate partner, allow them time to come around and decide what they want. They have free will and have every right to decide how much of their attention they want to give you.

You must be okay with this.

Sometimes people need a friend to talk to and just be heard. They don't need you to fix anything or give them any opinions, psychoanalysis, or unsolicited advice. Don't talk...just listen. This is called being a sympathetic listener. It's quite a paradox. Usually, we want to rush in to rescue them. It seems counterintuitive to just be quiet and not try to fix anything. Lending an ear and being present is all that is needed in these situations. This type of interaction borders on being a sacred exchange because you are accepting the person as they are, and witnessing their struggle without judging them.

I've contemplated where my path is heading and I've realized I want to just *be there* for them. I want to be able to just listen and witness what is on their mind. I don't think men want unsolicited advice or that they even understand the concept of support (I think of jockstraps and bras when I hear that word). What feels right to me is to just be there. Just listen and if someone wants my advice I will share it.

Lover Distortion Number One—Doesn't Express

This may seem blatantly obvious, but expressing your love to someone *is* a form of love. This is hard to do for some of us. I grew up in a family where we did not say "I love you" to each other very much. I'm not calling my family loveless, but I do know most of my life there was a certain uneasiness I had around saying "I love you" to people. And rarely could I process what it meant when people told me they loved me. You could say I had a hard time feeling the love being expressed by others. The good news is, as I've grown emotionally, all the anxiety around saying and hearing *I love you* has vanished.

Speaking of not saying *I love you* very often, one distortion of patience is when a person doesn't express what they want. Besides potentially being a worthiness issue, some people don't express what they want out of frustration. Maybe the result of being let down over and over makes the person so frustrated they figure the effort needed to describe their wants takes longer than just doing it themselves. This is a very destructive dynamic hurting many marriages because it leads to resentment. If one partner just gives up on their spouse, it creates a lot of tension and power struggles.

I saw this happen many times with my ex-wife. She would get frustrated if I didn't do something quick enough or perfectly. Debbie got to the point where she would say, "well I don't even ask because you're not going to do it the right way, and it's going to take more effort for me to ask for your help versus just doing *it* myself."

What I Did Before

This happened to me with my first web design business. I hired a young artist who was very talented yet often had the propensity to go in a different direction than what I asked. He was very creative, and what he delivered was usually great. But almost as often, to get the project back on track from the tangents he pursued would cost a *lot* of time. My dilemma was how to best use my resources. I could do the production work myself or pay someone to do it for me. Eventually, I had to let him go because working with him was ultimately too inefficient. Sadly, with a little more seasoning I think he would have really helped my business accelerate. In hindsight the lesson I learned is that I was probably being a little too impatient.

What I Do Now

I am now opening myself up to receive help. I tell myself if I don't ask for help, I may be closing myself off from the support and assistance people are willing to give me. I remind myself that I may be denying the other person an opportunity to express themselves or contribute. I'm working on being more direct with people. I've hemmed and hawed around in the past and avoided getting to the point when, if I needed it, I asked for help.

How you communicate is especially important when it comes to bonding with your children. While you need to be clear that you're the parent and in charge, it's important to communicate with your child in a firm yet non-threatening way. It is also important for you to be patient and allow your child to share their needs from their perspectives. It is absolutely wonderful when you collaborate with your kids on projects. This is your reward for being patient and you don't just *do it yourself*. When you insist on doing things yourself you are robbing your child of the opportunity to grow.

When commitments and agreements aren't put in place and allowed to stick, emotions begin to fester and bitterness and hatred can result, becoming fertile ground for unseen tensions and a negative environment.

Many people go through life with issues expressing themselves because they've been in relationships where the other person was overpowering or constantly let them down. Whatever the case is, remember to express yourself and what you desire, and allow the other person to do the same.

Lover Distortion Number Two—Control Issues

It's easy to connect the dots to see how not being patient and a need to control situations relate. I've been around people like this most of my life. Hearing statements like "I need this right now," or "I need this done like this," or "Why can't you help me *now!*" or "Why can't you just do what I say?" are negative things said by people who need to have control. I think this originates obviously from a lack of patience, but it goes to another level, and like so many of these extremes, having control issues seems to relate to a scarcity mentality.

Being patient is about allowing people to do what they are going to do. It is about creating the space for things to show up and unfold naturally, and being okay with other people's input without trying to control everything. It's about letting people experience and do things their own way. However, people screw up and it's easy to get frustrated when we are attached to a certain way we think something needs to be done. *Control freaks* have a specific outcome in mind and can sometimes be difficult to work with if you see things differently (think Meryl Streep in *The Devil Wears Prada*).

Control issues can also show up when people struggle with accepting themselves. This could be related to how one feels about their physical appearance and not liking what they see in the mirror. Whether it is one's weight, hair, wardrobe, skin, or anything else related to self-image.

Also the *control freak* expects external things to be perfect. They want their house to look a certain way, their kids to be spectacular, their spouse to *do* things a specific way. It shows up in the workplace too. Living this way can be exhausting and takes up a ton of energy.

What I Did Before

I remember one day I was with a friend named Becky having coffee in the Valley at Kaldi's talking about my soon to be ex-wife and Becky said, "You've got control issues." Her point was in order to see Deb as controlling, I too had to have control issues so I could recognize her behavior. I was blown away. I was like "Are you high? I'm a super-chill, mellow, let-people-do-whatever-they-want, Zen kind of dude." How would I ever be someone with control issues? It was like she was speaking a foreign language, and so I of course took control over the conversation and changed the subject!

Shortly after this, another friend of mine was in town. She's a personal development coach who knows a lot about relationships and I really respected her and valued her advice. Her name is Tori, and we were hanging out in Webster Groves having a late lunch, and I said, "Can you believe Becky told me I have control issues?" Tori's reply was, "Well, you do!" I was like "Wait, are you crazy too?" I started laughing and she reiterated "You do," and said, "Own it, just embrace it, and know it's okay, and people who are in control get things done." And then she said "Look, you have a team of people working for you, and you're the boss. You need to be in control to be the leader of your team." She went on to explain control is a very positive thing.

I sat with all this a while and processed what Becky and Tori said. These two friends are very intuitive and it was a blessing that they pointed this out to me.

I then realized I must have been projecting energy around my own control issues and as a result I kept perceiving *others* as being the *control freaks*. Ultimately I needed to learn about control.

At the root of my control issues were *daddy issues.* Because I had issues with my Dad and how domineering he was, I developed a more passive personality and let other people have all the control in most situations. I also had some passive-aggressive behaviors going on a little too because I confused people trying to be in control with trying to overpower others, and so there was a part of me that rebelled.

The next weekend I was at a family function where my sister-in-law was having a get-together. Normally I'd watch her *bossing* her husband and kids around and it would make me uptight. It would affect me so much at times I'd have to go to another room because it reminded me of my wife bossing me around and I didn't like how I felt under her thumb all the time.

After Tori told me to embrace my control issues, this family gathering was totally different. I was blown away by how the get-together felt. I think it was Easter Sunday when my perspective shifted. Now what I was seeing was my sister-in-law working really hard to ensure everyone had a great dinner, and all of this was coming from a place of love. She enlisted her husband and kids to do their part to help in the process. Nothing more or nothing less. I didn't feel any of my usual angst. When I realized I was the one assigning a meaning to what I was seeing and that I could control my reaction. After this aha moment I couldn't do anything but laugh. I was so giddy when I realized how amazing it was to experience things in a new way! I was so excited I called my friend Tori, and I left a voice message saying "I am a control freak and *I love it!*"

I think we cause self-inflicted pain when we try to control people and think they're supposed to do things a certain way, and when they don't, it can be agonizing. This relates to thinking there are only so many things out there to acquire so *stuff* needs to be perfect. In actuality, we are only just hurting ourselves and it has nothing to do with other people.

What I Do Now

The answer was to accept my control issues and to understand their blessings. Once I accepted having control didn't make me a jerk or hinder my creativity, it no longer had a negative triggering effect on me and the pattern seemed to dissolve. I've also accepted people's need to control situations. I now realize this is just their current stage of development and I have faith all people continue to grow.

A breakthrough I just had the other day was to embrace an entirely new level of self-control. I realized what happened in the past regarding control had to do with two things: First thing: I perceived people trying to control me. A lot of people tell us what we should be doing, and on an innate level, this feels like our free will is being trampled on. I know I have held this belief most of my life.

Secondly, "It takes one to know one" — I too know how to manipulate and control others and I no longer want to be this way.

I figured out what really mattered was that I needed to learn better *self-control* in order to have more integrity within myself. I now better understand myself and what I value. This breakthrough has enabled me to go easy on myself and accept who I am right now.

This is what we're going to talk about in the next chapter.

Rider Reminders

- We are always having our patience tested.
- Take one situation at a time to strengthen your patience muscle.
- Patience and great communication are the foundation of every successful relationship.
- The ideal attributes of the Son and Warrior help you become more patient—for instance, the calm and discipline you develop as a warrior helps you become a more patient lover.

Chapter Ten—What No One Taught Us

> *"Today you are you! That is truer than true! There is no one alive who is you-er than you! Shout loud, 'I am lucky to be what I am!' "* —Dr. Seuss [13]

Lover Ideal Number Two—Self-Love

I'm going to try to help guys get a little more dialed in on what self-love is all about. We are bombarded by messages that say love is *out there* somewhere. We feel like a void is created inside of us when we're alone and it needs to be filled with someone or something. The one big takeaway I want you to get from this book is that this perceived void is an illusion, and we dudes are whole already, whether we have an "Easy Lover" or not.

How do we fill this void? We fill it by accepting and loving who we are first. This starts with how we talk to ourselves. We have this recording playing all the time in our heads and we beat ourselves up more than we realize.

The thing I replace this negativity with now is self-forgiveness and mercy.

Incidentally, I was making coffee just now and dropped a mug on the kitchen floor and it shattered into a hundred pieces. In the past I would have been pissed at myself for doing this, but I am happy to report, instead I just marveled at how all the pieces splattered everywhere and all their shapes and sizes. What is the point of getting upset over something as trivial as a broken mug?

The root of self-love is accepting your current circumstances. You have to be okay with how the thousands of choices you've made have landed you *perfectly* right where you are at this moment. This is about taking a deep breath and saying to yourself "well then, how's it going bro?" and being perfectly fine with the answer. And loving yourself anyway, and being excited for what you have, and where you are heading.

Incidentally, self-love is also about realizing we don't need the acceptance of others. I mentioned this was the pain point of the Son. Self-love is such a foundational characteristic and many healthy things can spring from it, but as men, we aren't given many examples of what self-love is.

A great model of how self-love looked was personified by my Father-in-law Bob. He is probably the first guy I met who outwardly displayed self-love. One excellent consequence of his self-love is how his children turned out. Each of his four kids has very high self-esteem and standards for their lifestyle. Bob taught them to not settle. One way he did this was by teaching his kids when they were buying things it was always smart to get the best quality they could afford at the time. It was great advice because it helped them not have cheap standards, saved them money in the long run, and illustrated to them they were worthy of having the best if it was within their means.

While I never witnessed it, Deb told me her Dad used to stand in front of the mirror and say to himself "You look BEEEE-YOU-TEEE-FUL!" I chuckle at this now when I think about it. I can just see him standing there in his white v-neck t-shirt, slicked back thinning hair with his belly protruding a little as he looked at himself in the mirror as he was saying this. I must admit the first time she told me this story my self-esteem was very low and I didn't really know anything about self-love. Frankly, I thought it was kind of embarrassing and even a little repulsive when I first heard this.

Now, however, when I think about him (RIP Bob) I think about our close relationship and how he left behind a legacy of confidence and self-worth to his family. It occurred to me what he may have been sharing with his kids was to just be themselves. When I think about it now I realize beauty is really being you. I can now hear Bob's voice saying to me "You look BEEEE-YOU-TEEE-FUL!" Ain't nothing wrong with this sentiment! That may sound boastful or self-indulgent but what I'm getting at is that everyone is unique and beautiful in their own way and discovering what is beautiful about yourself is at the crux of self-love.

But how do you get to this degree of self-love? Unless you had someone modeling this to you, this rarely happens overnight. We have a lifetime of bullshit to unload and let go of. You can look at positive quotes and memes on Facebook for hours on end, or you can go see a counselor who listens to you and tells you to "breathe through it" and to "feel the feelings." I think there is a lot more to this situation and I believe the habit of loving yourself is an ongoing process. It's like an excavation project featuring a series of "Aha" moments that help you shift as you dig through memories.

Self-love can also be the result of taking the time to create new habits. We can add new routines to support our adventures by incorporating things like exercising, yoga, breathwork, praying, eating better, and journaling. These practices are pretty popular these days and talked about by many coaches and teachers.

In my opinion, I think we need to take action consistently and form habits around improving our health in order for self-love to truly take root.

What I Used To Do

For most of my life, I didn't really have boundaries and I was a close talker. I can remember a few times at college parties I'd literally talk people into a corner and not even be aware of it until there was nowhere the person could go. A big lesson I learned over time was there seems to be a correlation between my self-worth and my lack of boundaries.

During what I called my *awakening phase* I started to learn how to not let people's words and the intentions behind them (the energy I was feeling) affect me.

When I started to respect myself more it was really a shock for my wife because she outright wasn't used to it. She had been very accustomed to the people pleaser who I had been the majority of our marriage. In hindsight, she was just being herself and I can't really be mad at her Type A behavior.

What I Do Now

As I learned to recognize people projecting their issues, I wasn't manipulated by others as much anymore. I was taking on more Warrior energy finally and I stood up for myself more often and learned that I get to pick how available I want to make myself to others.

There are acceptable ways for people to interact with me and I get to pick if I will allow certain interactions or not.. We are taught to avoid conflict and to stay humble but we shouldn't allow people to walk all over us. Self-love helps us to stick up for ourselves, basically.

Another example is when you can say "I love myself enough to be mindful of how people treat me."

What we expect from ourselves is related to how we teach people to treat us.

Here is a list of things I consider related to building our esteem and self-love:

- Not putting ourselves down
- How we let others talk to us and treat us
- The level of physical health we settle for
- Our appearance and hygiene reflect a standard of self-worth
- How clean we keep our surroundings
- How we prioritize our time
- The type of food we eat
- How much we let others interrupt us or control our time
- Our income level, and our thoughts and actions around finances
- How we interact with our kids
- How much sleep we get
- If we allow ourselves enough time to exercise
- How much downtime we give ourselves to learn new things

It is important to remember everyone is allowed to choose what is important to them. Other people's values have nothing to do with *our* worth.

Several years ago, I inadvertently initiated a routine of self-love when I approached a fitness trainer to create a routine for me. One day before we started the program we met at a restaurant and the first thing she talked about was my self-love. I was floored. It was a foreign thought process to me at the time. Here was this person who I thought was going to be training me on working out, and the first thing she wanted to know about me was how much I loved myself!

She asked me outright "do you love yourself" and at that moment I had a really hard time answering. She made me put a sign in my bathroom which read "I love myself." She explained that I needed to get used to looking in the mirror and saying, "I love myself. "When I got used to this she instructed me to say "I love myself because _____" She had me write down reasons why I loved myself and to get used to looking in the mirror and saying "I love myself because I'm a nice person" and "I love myself because I'm a good dad and a good son." This was kind of cool and she said when you get comfortable with this I want you to add one final piece which was "I choose_____." And so she said it goes something like "I love myself because I work hard (or whatever those reasons were) and I choose _____." ("I choose happiness"… "I choose abundance…" etc.)

While this took a while and was a process, this is how I began learning to love myself.

In a nutshell, in order to be loved by others, we have to have enough love to give. Ideally, you want to be overflowing with love for yourself, so you have plenty to give other people.

Lover Distortion Number Three—Unworthy

Our parents are the earliest models we have of what love looks like and this may be good or bad. Even though my dad was really strict with us kids, he was very much in love with my Mom. I enjoy telling people the story about how my dad used to hug my Mom in the kitchen and often slide his hands down the back of her pants. Thinking of that totally cracks me up.

In addition to our family, we look to mass media to try to clue us in on what love is. One of the things we're exposed to is movies depicting a lot of over-romanticized and sexual B.S. Don't even get me started on all the fake B.S. on social media. And then when we turn on the radio or fire up our Spotify, all the songs we hear seem to be about being hurt or worrying about losing someone. Or they are about breaking up and making up, and all these *I'm not worthy* and *she's out of my league* thoughts that just seem to permeate our being because we're surrounded by this depressing energy. It's really crazy. I guess the broken-hearted artists get all the airtime.

On a side note, my best musical creations so far have come when I was in a really broken place.

Two questions we should ask are "What is one of the big reasons why we don't have enough self-love in our life?" and "Why do we have poor quality relationships?"

One answer has to do with worthiness and shame. Most of us had something happen in our childhood that caused us to experience the emotion of shame. A cascading effect results if the trauma ends up being unresolved.

At one point something happened to us as a kid and then the byproduct was a sense of unworthiness, shame, guilt, or even feeling dirty. This could have been triggered by countless things. Maybe your Mom said, "Shame on you for picking on your sister." Or the nun at school cracked your knuckles with a ruler for looking down a girl's shirt. Or you got busted sneaking your dad's *Playboys*. Maybe a friend made fun of your clothes or the car your parents drove. Or a coach was disgusted with you because you struck out at a pivotal time in a baseball game.

Shame is such a powerful tool and it's used to manipulate and control people.

What I Did Before

The problem with shame is it creates a recording on our soundtrack that makes us doubt our worth, and this can manifest distortions in our adult lives. For example, this belief can spiral into the idea that other people are better than us. Frankly, I really think what no one taught us is how to understand our worth and this is why people are confused about self-love.

After my guru moved back to her ashram in Colorado I began working with a yogini named Dianna to help me restart my in-home yoga practice. One of the most profound things she said to me one day was "David, you really self-identify a lot based on what woman is in your life." I asked her to clarify her point a few days later, (I tend to react slowly and stew on stuff) and she said a lot of the value I have for myself, and how I identify with who I am, is determined by the women in my life or the ones I want to have in my life. The statement was profound yet so true because up until that point it seemed that I didn't really have a measuring device to understand my value.

Shortly after this conversation, I began to try to understand my value as a person and my purpose in the world.

What I Do Now

I now understand that my value as a person isn't attached to who I'm in a relationship with. What helped me really understand this was an experience I had a couple years ago.

I was pretty content to not be a "love seeker" for a while and told myself in a year or so I'd probably be ready. Hahaha… But at the end of 2019, I met an *out of my league* woman and some major amorous feelings resurfaced in me.

We met initially on Facebook and she liked how I was not like all the neanderthal suitors messaging her. I was very chill and wasn't always making sexual innuendos or trying to rope her in somehow. After a few weeks, we decided to go on a walk to get to know each other. What I told myself was that I was not going to get too sucked in because I was unclear on how available she was because she mentioned having an on-again and off-again boyfriend. I did want to meet her however because she seemed interesting and someone that I could learn a lot from.

One thing I feel is common with a lot of men is that they feel certain women are out of their league and in this particular situation, I wanted to challenge this long held belief that I had. My new friend's college degree was from a very prestigious university, her father was wealthy, and her ex-husband was a millionaire, and so she was clearly an upper echelon woman with a great pedigree.

The day we were going to meet for the first time, I had the following realization and I posted on my Facebook page: "Some things have nothing to do with you but are great teachers." This was a cryptic message to myself basically saying go have fun with this learning experience, and whatever happens, is about her and not me. If she rejects me or accepts me, it is all about her.

This outlook made my first meeting with her very relaxing and natural. We went on to develop a pretty strong connection. It was great because this crush acted like a catalyst for me. I got serious about my workouts and was inspired to get my income on track. She was truly a muse for me and got the chemicals and creative juices flowing and going inside of me.

This experience added some zing to my holidays that year. We had some fun and I think we each taught one another a few things, but ultimately, we figured it'd be best if we just stayed platonic friends,

I'm grateful because this festive little period really helped heal some of my issues around worthiness, and because of my initial mindset about her being a teacher it made it much easier to swallow the pill of returning to the friend zone with her.

After this little mini-relationship experience, I was content to go back to plan A which was to work on my health, my business, and being a good dad. I also contemplated what Dianna said about my self-identification. I started to wonder who I am, what my purpose is, and what my worth was to the world. The first thing to come to mind was the value I have to my kids as their Dad and our priceless connection. Then I thought about the worth I had to my customers because of the creative solutions I provided them.

Then I had a very profound breakthrough!

I thought about the idea that there are many people struggling with diseases and even pending mortality. These people could have a lot of financial wealth but sadly may not have the health to enjoy it. Our health really levels the playing field regarding our material worth. This really hit home for me and helped me understand all the invisible / non-physical things in my life that truly dictate what my worth is.

After that realization I asked myself "What is the currency used to truly measure our worth?" And then it dawned on me. A little voice in my head said, "Love is currency." I thought about it awhile and became so happy to have this breakthrough. I started to think about all the love I have in my life and how it shows up. I have an amazing relationship with my daughters and my Mom. I have a big family consisting of seven siblings and spouses who all love me (or kinda like me at least). I have a big group of guy friends that have been in my life for over 40 years. Heck, I'm even close to my ex-wife's family. I have women friends who let me blather on and on about wellness and philosophy. If love truly is the way to measure our worth, I am a very wealthy person.

When you start to understand how worthy you are, you begin to know that the *special* person you are attracted to isn't out of your league. When you lose the baggage around your worth and forget about being ashamed, you can start loving the glorious and divine person you already are!

Lover Distortion Number Four—Outside Validation

One aspect of self-love has to do with knowing love is an inside job. It's great when you figure out how worthy and lovable you are and understand you don't really need anything outside of yourself to feel love. Read that again because it is such a rare idea. You don't need any *thing* outside of yourself to feel love. You can generate feelings of love on your own.

What I Did Before

In the past when I'd wonder about what was missing from my life, this illusion caused me to think I needed all these outside things to feel loved. This catapulted the need for validation into full swing. I'd often think about how it would be really nice if I could roll over in the middle of the night and have a warm body next to me to cuddle up to when I'm freezing after kicking all the covers off the bed. And at times, I really liked the idea of having a beautiful woman by my side to admire and to show off to my friends.

The world can really do a number on us and hypnotize us into feeling we need all this physical stuff in our life. A wife who is gorgeous and in great shape, the 3000+ square foot house, the new car, the kids who act perfect, the nice clothes, etc. etc.... These are beliefs our capitalistic society pounds into our psyche. It's great for corporations but not so great for us.

We want to be whole, but unfortunately, we leave off the *w* and all we feel is a *hole* we think needs to be filled.

What I Do Now

The good news, though, is that we can eventually get to a level of self-love where we figure out what makes us feel blissed out and what gives us joy. We understand how to do these mood-altering things all by ourselves. We discover that we don't need someone to fill this perceived void. All of those urges for outside love can be transmuted into feelings we can literally generate inside of ourselves all on our own. These amazing feelings can be accessed simply by remembering joyful moments in our life. Maybe it is a certain song or type of music which whisks you away to another time and brings back memories. Or maybe it is a physical sensation you have when you are really going for it during a workout.

For me personally, there are smells I encounter from time to time that stop me in my tracks and remind me of beautiful moments in my life. For instance, the smell of fresh coffee brewing reminds me of my grandpa because he used to tell me if I drank coffee my hair would turn dark like my big brother Mike. Whenever someone first lights a cigarette, that smell reminds me of my dad when he'd light a cigarette when we played *Midnight Monopoly* after he got home from working the 2-11 shift at the power plant.

There is an internal feeling of *realness* to all of those things, and these emotions aren't being generated outside of us by a romantic partner. You can add the *w* to your hole and feel fulfilled and happy when you break out of the illusion that the only way to feel complete is by having a woman by your side.

Feelings of joy, bliss, love, and excitement can be self-generated if you stop being so numb. You can tune into how things are going and ask yourself what makes you feel good, and listen to your inner voice. It will give you the answers. And, whatever this voice says, do more of that. I believe there are a lot of distractions that keep us feeling numb. I would like to challenge you to have periods when you turn off your cellphone and social media. I have made a conscious decision to limit my precious time to log on. This has helped me manage the feelings of needing outside validation. It has also freed up more time for me to spend outdoors to get fresh air and think more clearly.

What I Did Before

I struggled with validation issues right after my divorce. I think this is pretty common with most divorced men. I had a feeling something was missing from my life, and I had a void that I needed to fill and felt I could do that with a new woman in my life. I had to prove to myself a woman could still want me in a sexual way.

I think one of the biggest issues recently divorced men go through is the need to know that they are still desirable and this spawns from the Son's need for attention. Also, a lot of the issues newly divorced men have is related to needing to figure out their new post-husband identity.

We put a lot of pressure on ourselves trying to be sexy, cool, have great hair, and lots of muscles. All this is driven by ego and not Spirit. It doesn't help matters when we are in the checkout line and pick up a *"Cosmo"* for some intel on how the fairer sex thinks only to read about how imperative it is for women to have the ultimate orgasms. Then we think to ourselves, "If I don't perform, some guy with a bigger pecker and more money is going to come along and steal *my* woman." It's freaking brutal. Or worse yet, if you don't *have a woman* you begin to fear you'll never get one because you won't check off all the boxes women have for their perfect man.

One way I created self-inflicted pain around the sense of a void was by having an "if/then" mentality that went something like, "If I lose 25 pounds, then I can have a hot girlfriend," or "If I can make X amount of money and can buy a new house, then I'll be happy." This mentality is very limiting and blocks our manifesting abilities. It can really taint our reality because it perpetuates our belief that we aren't enough, and something is missing. We perceive a hole, and we need to fill but we never can!

I went through a phase of dating right after my divorce. Even though I told myself I was *awake* I wasn't aware that this need for validation was playing in the background. I needed to know if I could still attract a hot woman and turn her on. I had been with the same woman for 25 years so I naturally wondered to myself "Can I still satisfy a woman sexually, and can I get women's attention on social media or make new women friends? Can I make the librarian blush when I flirt with her as I paid the fine for my overdue books?" Then I wondered "How many women can I get to interact with me on dating apps?" Essentially I felt I needed a woman to make me feel fulfilled and whole again.

What I Do Now

You may be asking, "How am I supposed to manage this need for validation?" The first step for me was becoming aware of what it felt like when I perceived a void and when I felt like I needed someone outside of myself to fill it. My big breakthrough was when I remembered that I could observe myself from *outside of my head.* I recalled all the lessons I learned when I read Eckhardt Tolle's book *Power of Now.* I know for a fact his book massively changed my life.

My first *observe your mind* experience happened several years ago. At the time I was in the corporate world and I managed a team of about six people. I was the head of the creative department and we did work for about thirteen divisions of a big conglomerate here in St. Louis.

One morning I was lying in bed grieving how my morning at work was going to play out. I imagined how much of a mess it was going to be when I got to the office. I pictured a scene where my copywriter would arrive before me and she would roll her eyes and be sarcastic because everybody was late. And then we'd have a lot of pressure on us in the morning to get the ads we didn't finish on Friday done before 11:30. My senior graphic designer Shean would be his super casual self and come rolling in late while my junior designers would be doing their usual immature antics as we waited for the whole team to assemble. And my web guy Robert... well Robert would just be Robert.

This little pity party just went on and on and my thoughts literally made me sick. I felt depressed and helpless and had all this performance anxiety well up in me while I laid in bed. This scenario had happened many times on Mondays, but on this particular morning, I had a sudden realization that it was all just in my head. I said to myself "Look at what your mind is doing... look at the emotions this mind of yours is stirring up." I had an "Aha" moment when I realized I could become the *Observer*. I remember being really excited while I showered as I thought about my new superpower. The idea of catching my emotions before they spiraled out of control was such a liberating and exciting feeling!

How is this related to being able to fill a void or overcoming our need for validation? I believe our ideal state is when we're able to stay present and tap into the *Observer*. If you can observe what you do to yourself, and how you talk to yourself, and how you create either an upward spiral of positive happy energy or a downward spiral of oppressive feelings, this awareness can be pretty amazing. This ability is definitely a useful tool you can use when you feel like something is missing from your life, or if you feel like you need something to validate your worth. You can catch what your mind is doing and control your emotions before they go into a downward spiral.

In addition to being the *Observer*, I kind of reverse-engineered the *filling the void* situation. I thought to myself: "What are the feelings I have when an attractive woman interacts with me in the gas station line or a woman likes one of my posts or when someone attractive friends me on Facebook?" I asked: "What is it I'm feeling in those exact moments?"

And then I got quiet and remembered the sensations those scenarios caused me to feel inside. I realized that when I got that type of outside attention, it was like an adrenaline rush and a feeling that I was alive and it felt exciting.

I then asked myself: "What is something I do when I'm alone that has a similar feeling?" I realized I get those uplifting feelings sometimes listening to music, and I get those feelings driving in my car on an open road, and I feel it after a tough workout, or when I have a client tell me how happy they are with my work, or when a big check shows up in the mail. I also get those sweet feelings when I think about the awesome connection I have with my daughters.

Solving this need for outside validation was about knowing what makes me feel ecstatic and knowing I can generate those feelings for myself.

You can do this too by recognizing what helps you feel good and doing more of those things. Listen to loud music. Crank Eddie Van Halen's guitar solo on full blast. Do what gets you excited and feeling *epic*.

In summary, when we start to practice self-love we begin to evolve and realize the relationship we have with ourselves influences so many things. We stretch and become a new version of ourselves when we let all the self-judgment dissolve. And it's a beautiful thing.

When the need for outside validation dissipates, we're ready for the next level of love, which is the ability to love without reciprocity. I talk about that in the next chapter which is about being *unattached*.

Rider Reminders

- There's no guarantee that you are going to receive love from people and things outside of yourself. Self-love is an inside job and the only thing you have control over.
- Self-acceptance is the root of self-love.
- Our worth is not determined by material things; rather, it's by the amount of love we have in our life.
- Self-love is beyond boundaries. It's about loving yourself enough that you can commit to growing.

Chapter Eleven—Addition Through Subtraction

"When you are no longer tied to the outcome of how it must be, you free yourself up to abundant possibilities." —Shannon Kaiser[14]

Lover Ideal Number Three—Unattached

It is human nature to have expectations and to think love needs to look a certain way on the outside and we might even be owed something from our partner. People say things like "if you really loved me you would do ____." However, no one *ever* wants to be told what to do. We want options. We want things to consider.

In our confusion about love, we make up this picture of what it should look like and how people *should* treat us. Ironically, all these images about what love is supposed to look like were probably planted by some movie we saw when we were a kid. A two-dimension fake picture on a screen has filled our life with angst and turmoil. How's that for a bunch of cow manure?

My friend Tom's dad says, "Take care of yourself and the rest will take care of itself." Part of this is about self-love, and the other big part is about not putting expectations on others.

Many people are familiar with the concept of unconditional love as being a *higher* version of love. If a couple can accept each other and love one another unconditionally, that's great. I don't think this is the highest form of love though. It seems to me each person is just accepting their partner for who they are. They're accepting their partner's limitations and loving them anyway (or putting up with them).

Unconditional love feels kind of quid pro quo to me. It feels like the couple is saying to each other "I expect you to love me with all my faults because I love *you* with all of *your* faults." This is fine, but the minute one of the partners gets sick of the other's b.s., it all goes out the window. There seems to be a surrendering or compromising energy that would be hard to sustain.

I feel there is another level that is even more expansive than unconditional love. The idea of loving unattached seems to be a more evolved version of love and can be applied to all areas in our life. This is about doing acts of kindness without needing reciprocity. We talked about equal exchanges earlier and how important being in integrity with yourself is, but loving without expecting something in return is more like a virtue. It feels different than unconditional love to me.

In the Hebrew tradition, anonymous giving is considered the most honorable thing to do. No recognition, notoriety, or special favor is expected—you're just giving from a place of love. There is a Sanskrit word *Seva* that translates to "selfless service." Unattached love feels this way to me.

Loving unattached to outcomes is a very mature way to love someone. And in the long run, it seems like a great way to avoid disappointment and heartache. If we could just focus on feeling good in any given situation and staying present, we might stop thinking about expectations (which are just future illusions we're projecting). This is a hard habit to break, but as you continue to grow you develop the capacity to love for the sake of love, no matter the situation.

You can be super-close with someone, and be their *best friend*, but cannot own them. What comes to mind is all the Valentine's Day candies I've eaten that say "be mine" on them. I mean really, can someone actually be yours? Can you own them? I ponder sometimes where the line is drawn between admiring and appreciating something beautiful and thinking that you can *own* it.

You might ask, "How do I shift into this non-attached form of love?" First of all this reminds me of the Sting song "If You Love Somebody Set Them Free." Everyone wants to have freedom and not feel constricted. No one wants to feel like they are being controlled. Don't try to contain the person you desire or try to make them *yours*. You can smother them with your insecurities, or you can choose to create space for feelings to develop.

Loving unattached can also have the feeling of addition through subtraction. It is similar to someone wanting to quit smoking. They have a hard time giving it up because of the joy and satisfaction smoking gives them. Smoking is their thing. They really don't want to quit because it feels like something is being taken from them. Then one day they realize they are actually adding to their life by not clinging to this habit. They shift because they know the quality of their life is going to improve and when they come to that realization, at that moment they achieve the ability to kick the habit.

When you realize something isn't being taken away from you and see from an unattached perspective, you're *adding* to the experience. I feel your partner will love you even more if they don't feel smothered.

What I Did Before

In the first chapter of the book when I talked about naivety, I mentioned my *lightworker* phase and how I felt part of my purpose was to put more loving energy out into the world. To some degree, I still feel that is part of who I am and hopefully other people feel the same way about their purpose. I'm a very loving person. I have a lot of friends and family that I like to check-in with. I like letting them know I'm thinking about them and on a pretty regular basis I outright tell them I love them.

The way I see it, sometimes life can be tough and by reaching out to people I'm helping them feel good. When someone receives a quick text affirming someone is thinking of them, I figure it helps, at least a little.

Occasionally, though, I really crave a sense of connection. If I'm struggling, sometimes I send out a handful of texts to check in with people and if I'm being totally transparent here, I'll admit that I'm sometimes hoping someone will reply back and say *"hi"* and mention they're thinking of me too. There's a really subtle intent to receive reciprocated attention back in those instances. This isn't always my intent, but it's there sometimes if I'm not in an ideal emotional state.

What I Do Now

Writing this book has been very therapeutic and I continue to learn and contemplate why I do what I do. Regarding this issue of messaging people, I realized this has to do with a bigger issue related to a need for connection. I asked myself: "Why is this so important to me?" and "Why does it matter if someone gets back to me?" What I realized eventually was that I still had a very deep form of loneliness at times and this was an attachment issue. With this new awareness, I really want to break free of it once and for all. I really really do care about people but I don't want to have expectations either.

People can sense when someone (myself included) has an almost desperate need to connect. There is a magnetism between people and everyone can sense it. If there are similar interests and temperaments you feel attracted to someone and you connect on an energetic level. However, when one person is trying too hard to connect it actually repels the other person.

So the big thing I do now is really check my intentions when I am trying to connect with people whether it is via text, social media, on a phone call, or in person. What I realize is that I may be trying too hard. The goal is to be neutral and not worry about getting attention or approval. I've gotten into the habit of checking my intention before I hit *Send* on a text. I'm to the point now where before I even compose a text to someone, I ask myself: "What am I inviting in here?" And if I'm looking for attention or validation, I stop myself.

The most impactful realization I had is that this attachment issue is about needing to connect to myself. A challenge happens for me when I spend a lot of time alone and it becomes difficult to handle isolation. I understand now that I have the capacity to love myself and I don't have to be attached to someone to feel complete.

I've realized that if I can practice non-attached love with my family and friends I will be okay if my perfect romantic partner doesn't show up right away. What I am working on now is just being in flow and in a state of *allowing* whatever is meant to show up as often as possible. I'm also learning that there is an incredible freedom to this way of living my life. It is like the shackles of needing outside validation have finally been removed because I'm no longer being a seeker..

Lover Distortion Number Five—Fear of Loss

When I contemplated the ability to love without an attachment, I had to think a bit regarding what the distortions of this would be. I began thinking about how, during most of my intimate relationships, deep down I feared I was going to lose the person.

What I Did Before

Sometimes I feel there is going to be *one* person who will fulfill me and when each of us is ready, we would, (as my *Law of Attraction* friends like to say) attract each other into our lives. When this magical time comes, we would be blissed out and content since we finally found our true love. As conscious as I thought I was, I didn't realize that buried under the surface I still had all this immature lover stuff like jealousy, attachment issues, anxiety, and relationship fears.

Even though I wasn't actively seeking my perfect person, here's what happened shortly after my *out of my league* partner and I decided to stay in our own lanes and go into the friend zone. A new *teacher* appeared on my radar two months later.

As a matter of fact, she's the person who encouraged me to write this book.

I was dropping off a USB drive to a business associate at a networking event. I was there only for a few minutes but on my way out, I ran into this new Facebook friend on her way in. When I realized who she was and introduced myself, I felt this bolt of energy shoot through me like I'd never felt before. Shortly after that electrifying encounter, we agreed to meet to see what potential business synergy existed between us. When we met officially for coffee, within about a minute, I could tell we had some magnetism between us, and about six minutes into our meeting I outright said to her I found her very attractive. I *never* act like this when I first meet a woman.

Even though our fling was rather short, it was a pretty amazing experience, and I learned a ton about myself over the course of four months. It was magical whenever we got together and it seemed like time didn't exist. I also really liked that it felt like we were on the same consciousness level.

One day she mentioned it appeared that I had an attachment to her. This was a very foreign idea to me at the time. I asked her to explain and said: "We obviously have a connection." She confirmed yes, we did indeed have a connection, and then went on to explain if one of the people in a relationship was afraid of losing the other person, or if a person had expectations the other couldn't necessarily meet, then this person had an attachment. It bothered me at first, but then I realized she was right and that I had begun imagining her possibly being *the one,* and in a subtle way, I did begin having a few worries of losing my *perfect* partner.

I was so busy being excited that I found someone who had the same experiences and temperament as me, and someone who was entrepreneurial with amazing energy, that I was blinded to the fact that I did indeed have an attachment. I then went on a mission to prove I didn't! I gave her a ton of space and did my best to not come across as being too needy. Unfortunately the perception was that I had an attachment and so the damage was done.

What I Do Now

I recognized a pattern of insecurities that I have that causes me to fear I'm going to lose my romantic partner. Just having this realization is a big first step for me. I really did some soul searching after my last relationship to learn more about this *fear of loss* theme on a deeper level.

I realized that I was evolving past my fears of being worthy and that my need to be validated by a woman was diminishing. But this fear of losing an intimate partner lesson seems deeper, as if it's some sort of survival instinct. I kept asking myself: "What is this fear of loss about?"

I can certainly tell you these fear of loss feelings seemed to happen in all of my significant relationships. No one wants to feel the pain of rejection, but this seemed deeper than that. In general, I think it goes something like this: when we are intimate with someone who we deem to be our *perfect* lover, it feels like we're finally home and we don't want to leave. We want the nights we have together never to end. These are such amazing feelings we don't want to let go of them because our emotional connection to this person is so strong,

If anything, this *fear of loss* lesson is about the *illusion* of perfection. When we think we've found the perfect relationship, we want to latch onto it. But it *is* an illusion because literally, *there's no such thing as perfection in the physical world.* It's a ghost. All we see is an artifact of something that was there only for the briefest instant. In essence, what I'm saying is that if you can get to a state where you believe you don't *own anyone* then logic dictates there really isn't anything to lose if it wasn't yours in the first place.

After the intensity of that relationship began to wear off, it gave me an opportunity to replay in my head all the wonderful times I've had with platonic friends and intimate partners, which helped me realize I don't need to have anymore anxiety over whether the perfect person is going to come into my life. And with this acknowledgment, the fear of loss is starting to loosen its grip on me.

Lover Distortion Number Six—Obsession

While fear of loss is about worrying about a relationship ending, obsession happens when we're pursuing a person or object of our desire. It can also show up in our careers and parenting.

This distortion is about emotionally attaching too much to something we don't have.

The relentless pursuit of a desire is a powerful force. From a positive perspective, this *hell-bent, won't stop at anything,* energy can be pretty incredible if it's harnessed properly. Obsession can potentially help us *push through* when a project is coming down to crunch time. I think the drive to get in shape, or to get things done can improve with obsession energy, One thing I learned in the book *Think and Grow Rich* is that our work can benefit by refocusing sexual energy. If we can put that angst to good use in our business, this is great.

Obsession reminds me of the immature Warrior who wants to win at all costs and wants to do whatever it takes to conquer—and win over his lover. It almost seems like a heroic quality if a guy is obsessed with getting the girl of his dreams.

What I Did Before

I joined a couple of dating apps after my marriage. It started out of boredom and curiosity as to what's out there, but before long the obsession crazy train left the station and I got blown away by all the options on those apps. My brain was like "Wow, look at her and her and her and her..." and then escalated quickly to "Now, how can I get *her* attention?"

I'd connect with a woman and then I'd have to play the waiting game and wondered how quick I should reply? This kind of craziness went on and on. Then when we'd take it up a notch and begin to communicate outside of the dating app, the obsession would go to another level. I would obsess over texts, notifications, social media posts, likes, and comments.

There is so much information about women, and the accessibility to them now is crazy. It can occupy a single guy's brain 24/7.

What I Do Now

When I'm feeling whole and believing in myself I'm okay with whatever shows up in my life, I truly don't care how things are going to end up and I'm not in that *love seeker* mode. There's a certain liberation to this way of being and I realize those *obsessive* feelings have lost their grip on me. I can redirect the energy and time into more productive endeavors. When I realize I'm obsessing over things, I quickly catch it and calm myself. Oh and I deleted the dating apps!

I have a new rule for myself. One way I'm improving my obsessive behavior is to be aware of the number of times I think the same thought. A friend of mine who is an expert on emotions calls this *looping*. My new strategy is to allow myself to think about a particular situation or person only three times a day. This technique helped me get over the lover I was talking about earlier in this chapter. I now take one moment at a time and focus on the one thing in front of me to get done, and then do this over and over again.

I apologize if the stories in this section seem to be too self-indulgent. My hope is that the examples I share based on my recent relationships can demystify the craziness that goes through our heads when we chase after a romantic partner.

All this *doing the work* stuff can be exhausting. Hopefully, in our evolution, we are expanding our awareness and this is what the next chapter is all about.

Rider Reminders

- Obsession over dating can be avoided when we stay present.
- Loving without the need for reciprocity is the highest form of love.
- Nothing outside of yourself can fill your perceived void.

Chapter Twelve—SEX... Yes Please

*" We have only the present moment,
sparkling like a star in our hands — and
melting like a snowflake." —Marie Beynon
Ray* [15]

Lover Ideal Number Four—Sacred

I originally wrote this chapter right after the relationship with my *detachment* teacher ended. I learned so much about myself and relationship dynamics during that brief period, but I was also a little jaded at the time and felt I had something to prove to her and probably every other woman who chose not to be my *forever person*.

It recently occurred to me that this chapter read like a disjointed 5000 word *personals* ad and realized I wouldn't have been very authentic if I pretended to be some expert at romantic relationships. I have reflected on my love life quite a bit since then and now feel there are three areas I can authentically talk about regarding sacred partnerships.

The first area has to do with understanding how we become our sacred self, the second is what I call platonic intimacy, and the third topic has to do with sacred romance.

Sacred self–

At the end of the last chapter I mentioned that if we can manage our obsessions we can improve our focus. There is an emotional haze that gets lifted and you get really good at witnessing all the beautiful and wondrous things surrounding you. A new perspective can start to develop where you see how amazing, luscious, and intertwined everything is and a new degree of awareness unfolds and your senses are heightened. You begin to look at the world with awe like a child and move toward becoming sacred. You can intentionally slow down and become present and start to honor and respect people and all living things.

This reverent state of being affects all of our relationships and especially our romantic partnerships.

Consequently, becoming your sacred self is really about personal evolution versus the quest of finding a soul mate..

During our journey as a lover, we may eventually discover and pursue a spiritual path. We see the alpha and omega and realize there's always beginnings as well as endings. We also realize those endings can be destructive and knowing this, on some deep level, we can have a sense of surrender because we realize that at the end of endings, there are new beginnings. We then recognize our connection to this cycle of life and begin to experience things beyond the physical world courtesy of this new awareness. We can start to feel *The All That Is*. One may actually even call this behavior being *holy*.

The idea of becoming a holy man and embracing our sacred self sounds pretty similar to the concept of the divine masculine. A lot of coaches talk about the polarities of the divine feminine and divine masculine. I feel like that subject matter is a bit beyond my expertise and the scope of this book. My intent is to introduce ideas and hopefully guide men to become their best versions of themself.

I'd like to be really practical. I think it boils down to this: everyone is equal and we are all connected to an infinite source of life. We should strive to treat one another with respect and the highest form of love possible. If we understand our own value, we can start seeing the beauty and sacredness in others. To get to this level it requires evolving yourself first before worrying about being in a romantic partnership with someone else.

I feel this is why it's important to have practices that help you love yourself because it expands your capacity to give and receive love from others. If this practice makes the guy a divine masculine so be it. Instead, I'd call him a Whole Dude.

Platonic Intimacy–

There is a classic debate on if men and women can be *just friends* and I've spent a bit of time wondering about this myself because I probably have as many women friends as I have men friends. My answer to that question is that yes, men and women can just be friends if each person is honest with each other about what they want to get out of the relationship. Sometimes these friendships are simply about having companionship and someone to grab a coffee with or be your *plus one* at an event. Other times, we may be just needing the perspective of someone from the opposite sex or just be witnessed and bounce ideas off of someone. This isn't always easy to do with other men and so we approach women to have these more intimate interactions. These scenarios are innocent enough and don't need to lead to the bedroom.

The friendships I'm talking about here are with people who are beyond just acquaintances because there is indeed some type of connection, but it isn't necessarily sexual. These experiences that I've had with some fantastic women have been very enjoyable and I'd describe the exchanges as platonic intimacy.

I feel people are so very guarded these days because everyone has experienced being hurt by someone and so it takes a bit of trust building between people to have intimate exchanges. We are so sensitive to the feeling that people are trying to get something that we may not be willing to give and so we put up walls to block out being too close, too fast.

I've learned that sometimes I get too close to people too quickly and it seems a lot of people can't handle that and these close friendships sometimes fade as a result. I'm still working on finding this balance and sharpening my ability to navigate those relationships.

At a deep level each person is using their senses to determine if they will be safe with the other person. They are sensing if this person might hurt them and this can even apply to platonic friendships. People often create a barrier to a sense of connection to the opposite sex until they feel trust.

Intention is a very powerful thing. It is stronger than words. A guy can pretend he is okay being only friends with a woman, but if he is just waiting around for her to let her guard down and is going to put his moves on her when she is vulnerable, that is no bueno. Women that are evolved can sense his intention as subtle as it is. A good friend of mine named Natalie made a comment that described this perfectly and made me laugh hysterically. There was a self-described divine masculine in her yoga class that she said was trying to "Namaste, his way into her pants."

Once we confirm that we are safe and can let our guard down around someone, we can begin to truly learn about each other. In some way it may feel like we are a kindred spirit of sorts. A lot of new age people like to talk about finding their soul family and hanging out with their vibe tribe or being with someone who has the same frequency (as if it is a radio station each person is tuned into). Coaches like to think that their *vibe attracts their tribe*. I get that but I'm not into using those words because I don't think people really know what any of that means. This is really about being in phase with someone when their energy resonates with yours. I talk about this some in the *Understanding Energy* section in the Appendix.

Instead of frequency, I like to think more about synchronizing with someone else's time and movements as we do a sacred dance together. When a Wake Rider is surfing is he thinking about vibration and frequency? NO! He's feeling into the rhythm of the wake and coordinating his actions with the water. In a sense, he is even becoming one with the sea. The connection he has is undeniable and this union is a spiritual experience for him. He is adjusting and reacting to all the energy of the ocean as he is being carried forward to the shore. He is part of this flow and force that can be ecstatic and possibly terrifying at the same time. This is about sacred movements and not vibration or frequency and this is how I want to interact with intimate partners.

Sacred exchanges happen when two people can say "This is what makes me feel good and I hope you feel this way too." They don't tell the other person how they deserve this or that. The partners can safely open up to each other because they know they will honor each other's worth. There is a sense of reverence they have for each other.

I think this way of being with others helps create an environment where each person can safely learn about themself (and obviously the other person). I've received tremendous value from relationships where my friend affirms the new ideas I have and is open to share their feedback. As a matter of fact a lot of the material in this book is the result of lengthy conversations I've had with friends I consider sacred partners.

These conversations can take a lot of energy though and I now realize my friends don't always want to take long trips down rabbit holes. It is important for me to recognize that it isn't always okay to do this with my friends.

One thing related to this idea is unsolicited advice and a clash for attention. It bugs me sometimes when this happens. And as I've mentioned before, what I like about people I like about myself and what I don't like about people is what I don't like about myself. Meaning that when people are giving me unsolicited advice and it bugs me, it is a reminder that I do this to people too and don't like that part of myself.

I had to sit with this awhile to realize what was going on with me at a very deep level. I always assumed I was creating value for people, but then I realized I was giving unsolicited advice to people and sometimes I was hogging all of the attention in a conversation. I was being unethical. The exchange wasn't equal. Some people might not have wanted to hear what I was saying or to use their energy to listen. In essence I did not have their permission to fire hose them with a bunch of information, and then expect them to give their input on my ideas.

I realize now that there almost needs to be an agreed upon protocol to follow when I have deep conversations with these close friends. Some facets of this may include:
- Does my friend have the time and energy for such a conversation?
- It's important to check in with how they are feeling too
- Make sure there is give and take in the conversation
- Listen to them on a deep level and not just be waiting for my turn to jump in
- Be open to their feedback and criticism and there is no need to be defensive or think that I need to be right.

- If I have the urge to coach them on a point, ask them first if they want to hear it
- Try to tune into any boundaries my friend has around this conversation
- Be wholeheartedly appreciative of their friendship and the things they teach me.
- Realize that if I'm triggered by anything they say that this has to do with a deeper lesson that I haven't learned yet
- Always set the intention to provide them value too
- Realize whatever advice I'm trying to give them is advice I probably need myself

In this ideal scenario we are both consenting to the exchange of information and energy that we are sharing and this feels good for both of us.

A Facebook Live conducted by Larisa Stow helped give me the language I was looking for to describe this way of communicating. Larisa is one of my favorite musicians and at 11:11 everyday she does a Facebook Live broadcast. On this particular day she was talking about how she wanted to honor everyone in her WEvolution community and give everyone a voice and expressed the desire for a type of framework that would foster open and healthy exchanges of ideas. This really got my attention. She went on to talk about boundaries and consent. These two topics are a perfect transition into the next type of sacred partnership.

Sacred Romance–

There were times in my marriage that came very close, but I'm pretty sure that I haven't had a full on *sacred* love affair. Since the end of my marriage, I feel like I've been a little premature in attracting my *perfect* lover. I think the women I've been with up to this point have all been tremendous teachers, but none of the relationships reached the level of being truly sacred. Unfortunately, there has been pain involved, so I'm ready to take a bit of a break from my hopes of finding *the one*. What I know is that I am growing tremendously as a person and feel a sacred romance would build off of what I just mentioned about becoming sacred and platonic intimacy. What I also know is that I've had some pretty fantastic encounters and here is how they typically go down for me (and probably most men)..

At the beginning stages of our budding romance we feel 100% alive. All of our senses are firing on all cylinders. I love the sound of her voice and how she smells. I love how her lips taste like cherry chapstick and the feelings of her touch when I pull her in for an embrace.

Every moment with our new lover feels sensationally *sensual*! Those two words are quite interesting when you think about how they are related to who we are as beings. Essentially we have billions of sensors all over our body and in the beginning of romantic engagements our sensors are on overdrive.

How do we get to that place of ecstasy I mentioned in the introduction of the Lover section? Ultimately that happens by letting go of fear and knowing you will be safe with the person you desire. You are *so okay* with this person, you are even okay with taking all of your clothes off in front of them. You might even be brave enough to be naked in front of them without needing to turn the lights out.

But you can't get to this ideal state if you are in a place of fear, or worry. You can't be distracted by stuff on your mind like work, body fat, or bank account balances. You have to be 100% present and aware at that very moment. You can let go and drop all of your facades because in that moment you feel invulnerable. Fear doesn't exist at that moment. There are no boundaries because you have become one with your partner. All of this sensual activity ironically relies upon being CON-sensual. And consent my friend is what the rest of this chapter is about.

I played a little trick here by calling this chapter *SEX*. We all know about physical sex and want to get better at it. In this case, I'm saying S.E.X. stands for *Sacred EXchange*. People may be disappointed that this chapter isn't about a sure-fire sexual move or something, but loving your partner with your mind, emotions, body, and soul is going to lead to your ultimate and most sustainable sex life.

Everything in this book up to this point is leading us to become the best lover we are capable of becoming. Think about it: our sacred lover is going to want all of our ideal Wake Rider aspects such as integrity, honesty, fun, patience, courage, great communication, worthiness, etc. Practicing everything we talked about up to this point *will* help you be a great lover.

The physical stuff is great to have, but to me it all seems temporary and can fade as we age. Sacred love is what you are building in order to have a partner for eternity. I feel so strongly about this that I'm starting to think that every romantic relationship that isn't a sacred partnership is just an experiment that will end eventually. I'm trying not to sound so arrogant to imply that men shouldn't even try to be in a romantic relationship until they have learned all of the Son and Warrior lessons, but I'd like to at least suggest that you will be a better lover if you can embody the ideals of those Wake Riders.

I think each romantic relationship we have presents an opportunity to evolve and to understand love more. Thankfully our perspective changes courtesy of our experiences. When one relationship ends, we can feel hurt and confused. In the next situation, we tell ourselves how things are going to be different, and we think about all the wonderful traits we're seeing in our new partner. And when that relationship fades for whatever reason, we move on again and hopefully learn something from the experience. I'd like to think marriages can also evolve and grow as the betrothed continue to understand themselves, their partnership, and hopefully there is a big enough container for them both to grow.

I think a lot of marriages end because people have been discovering the idea that there is more to life than just winning at the achiever game. Many people yearn to break out of the social norms. The conventional life playbook looks like this:

Get a college degree, Drink some Moscato, get a great job, pour all your energy into your career, find the perfect mate, get married, drink some Chardonnay, buy the big house, take two vacations to decadent locations per year, and do as many weekend activities as possible with your best friends. Drink red wine. Have one perfect son and one perfect daughter and watch them grow and leave you and drink more red wine and then retire not only debt-free but with at least a cool Mil in the bank.

At least that is what the glossy magazines and videos are conditioning us to believe.

A lot of us are realizing there is more to life than this blueprint. Some people are looking at their life partners and realizing they are vastly different and experience a desire to fulfill their purpose in life and to help humanity.

We begin to think about being of service and making an impact in the world, or at the very least become a better example to our kids as to why we're even here in the first place. If these values don't match what our life partner wants, as uncertain and scary as it seems, the pain of staying in a dead-end relationship is worse than the unknown. We decide to end these relationships to set out on our own. This is not an easy decision to make and there are a lot of people that just stay in unfulfilling relationships because of this fear of the unknown.

As we grow and learn more about ourselves, a desire is sparked within us to not go on this journey alone anymore. We begin contemplating what it would be like to have someone in our life with similar energy and how exquisite and fulfilling it would be to start feeling the magic again of a romantic connection with someone on a deep level. But we aren't as naive as we once were and this time around we may be a little more guarded.

I've talked about the Warrior defining what he accepts and is in essence creating boundaries and standards for himself. Consequently, when relationship coaches talk about boundaries I think this topic is more of a Warrior issue instead of a Lover issue because boundaries seem prickly and stout and not very loving.

I was struggling to find language to describe the dynamic of needing to be able to stand my ground during a conflict in a sacred relationship, while not being too brittle or lacking flexibility in my position. I was feeling that sacred love could be open enough to not even need boundaries. I also know it is important to honor and respect my lover and to acknowledge what is acceptable to them.

I was really having a hard time explaining this until I heard Larisa Stow talk about the idea of having soft boundaries. She compared this to when you were a kid at the amusement park riding the bumper cars. The bumpers on the cars keep everyone safe and are squishy and soft. This idea helped me process a way to describe how partners can have bumpers like this which allow each partner to be their authentic self and not have the fear of getting hurt.

Sacred love allows the partners to co-create a spacious invulnerable container for giving and receiving. It provides some structure and evokes a sense of invulnerability. A lot of relationship coaches try to convince men that they need to be in touch with their feelings and be vulnerable enough to share them with their intimate partner. A new way that I'm framing this is that in a sacred romance you have a sense of safety and trust where you can drop the masks you have hidden behind and be your authentic self. It is the invulnerable container with agreements and consent that helps foster the capacity to drop the mask. You don't feel vulnerable in those situations. Another reason this happens is each person is truly mirroring back aspects of themselves to each other and each sees their unity.

Traditional relationships are about *me as I relate to you* and vice versa. Some people say we live in a world of polarities, however, this new sacred romance is about oneness and the *Us* being co-created by two whole people. Each person helps teach their partner and can enhance each other's beingness.

Something I've witnessed in my own relationships is how each person begins to take on the dominant characteristic of the other, and therefore very congruent energy develops in the relationship. This feels like being able to trust my intuition more and at times being on the brink of being telepathic with my sacred partners. As this begins to surface and unfold into existence, I think this is what a unitive state would feel like between two people.

In *"The Nine Stages of Ego Development,"* it is mentioned that the Unitive stage is considered the highest form of development and is only experienced by about 1% of the population. I see a parallel between being in a unitive state and sacred romance because each individual is whole and represents their own microcosm, and when they unite it represents the macrocosm with infinite potential. Neither individual could experience this alone.

This unitive state is reached because the sacred union creates a third entity. It is beyond the sum of its parts. I've been using the term *beyond wholeness* to describe this phenomenon.

Talking about sacred partnerships is very important in the evolution of the Whole Dude. As you've noticed most likely already, there is a progression that is taking place. I feel sacred love is rarely illustrated in our world and so I hope you can now see how it can be the bridge into finding your soul and understanding your true spiritual nature.

Lover Distortion Number Seven—Putting up walls

One of the distortions of a sacred partnership is when you aren't willing to create that *Us*.

Putting up walls to true intimacy can happen in two ways. The first is when someone is just not ready to pursue a sacred partnership. This person may be content with their life and doesn't really feel like they need anyone else. It is very easy to settle into routines and practices and enjoy the freedom to do whatever you want without a partner's input. In my case at this very moment, I'm very busy with my work and feel that it'd be unfair to commit to someone who would want something that looks like a traditional relationship.

The second way people put up walls is when they are in a relationship already, but they aren't going *all-in* for some reason or another. Perhaps this is the result of past hurts experienced in other relationships. In this scenario, a sacred partnership isn't attained because both people aren't committed to the third entity. The oneness created by total openness, honesty, and 100% commitment to each other is never realized.

What I Did Before

This showed up for me in the relationship I was in that lasted three years. My post-matrimonial relationship was very loving and there were times we connected on a very deep almost soul level. I thought she was my forever person. I knew she had a drinking problem, but I felt it was part of my life's purpose to help her heal.

What ended the relationship wasn't the drinking issue (although it *was* a big part of the uncoupling because it cast a shadow of mistrust). What ultimately ended the relationship was all the other things that triggered me. At the top of the list was how she let her kids and ex-husband treat her, and the effect this had on our *Us*. As a result, I only emotionally committed 90%—I didn't go all in, telling myself I'd be shattered if I went all in and the relationship ended.

I look back at this now and see the perfection behind me putting up walls. The reason I say this is because I have grown so much in the years that followed that relationship. My intimate partner had very limited and conventional beliefs that I know I would have outgrown. I would have only been focusing on the physical aspects of myself.

In many ways this was an immature relationship with tainted beliefs and a slew of emotions based on an old paradigm. Things like lack of self-control, manipulation, projection, jealousy, blaming, and fear poisoned any chance this could have turned into a pure, sacred partnership.

Putting up walls is about protecting yourself from potential hurt. It's the act of not fully trusting your partner out of fear they'll reject or hurt you somehow.

What I Do Now

I propose we take a break from our fears of being hurt and for a moment contemplate the concept of the couple being *invulnerable*.

My vision and what I truly desire is to become one with the other person, and in the oneness we realize we are each other's perfect teacher. We reflect back parts of ourselves that need to be acknowledged, whether deemed good or bad, light or dark, shameful or glorious. We'd lovingly facilitate this for each other, sometimes inadvertently and sometimes deliberately.

This ideal relationship is so far beyond simple physical attraction. In some ways, this is your soul being able to see itself. In essence, intimacy = *Into Me I See.* In such a state of wholeness, the concept of being hurt or vulnerable does not exist because you both have grown to the most evolved way of loving each other. If you put up walls you will never witness this.

Lover Distortion Number Eight—Unfaithful

The most obvious example of *not* having a sacred romance is infidelity. In my heart of hearts I think infidelity in a relationship starts when you are unfaithful to yourself. You have failed to understand what is important to *you* and have started to get lost. In the process of not being faithful to yourself, most likely you've stopped communicating effectively with your partner or at the very least you settle for less than what you want.

Being unfaithful is such a major subject and there are so many examples we could go into about someone cheating on their partner, but I'm trying to look at this from a non-judging perspective.

I really think infidelity isn't just a spontaneous thing that happens. I think the sanctity of a relationship dissolves due to a series of disappointments. Or a void between the two partners is somehow created, and if we understand physics, we know the universe is going to fill it with something. You would think we could understand the fine line between infatuation and possession, and allowing and freedom, but without clear communication, it's really a gray area.

In a healthy relationship, each person understands how fragile connections can be and the importance of excellent communication skills. There's a very fine line between having agreements you lovingly communicate with grace versus feeling *deserving* and *getting something* from your partner. I can't emphasize enough how important it is to be able to shift away from this way of thinking and operating. When you can let go of this way of being, you set the tone and create a foundation for healthy and non-manipulative communication.

I think when a relationship is based on conditions and expectations, it can get dicey. Someone gets disappointed if they feel like their needs are not being met. The problem gets magnified when this person doesn't express their desires. I think the key is to communicate and provide guidance for each other as to what feels good for one another.

I think infidelity happens first by not being true to yourself regarding what is important to you. Understanding what is important to each other and doing the best you can to live your values is the ideal way to be. And then it's important to affirm these values with your partner.

When you're unclear on what you want or don't have, it will probably lead to one partner completely shutting down. It's also important to know your worth as a human and your role in the partnership—if you don't know this, you'll eventually lose the ability to feel appreciated.

I think when we are tempted to cheat it is because we feel like something is missing and we might even feel like our life is slipping through our fingers. We might even feel like the grass is greener on the other side of the fence. A remedy for this is to really figure out what you want. Your partner isn't a mind reader (at least not yet). Being able to know what you want and knowing how to gently talk about this goes a long way.

It really hurts though when things don't turn out the way we'd like. Sadly, pain (self inflicted even) is what we use to justify our infidelity. In some ways, it's like we're getting back at the other person for wasting our time. However, two wrongs don't make a right. And two darks don't make light. Admittedly when you don't know what you want it can be confusing as hell.

Society tells us someone who is unfaithful cannot be trusted and once a *cheater*, always a *cheater*. I don't think it is as simple as this. I think the topic of infidelity is complicated. I'm not proclaiming to be an expert, but my gut tells me infidelity seems to come from a place related to standards not being met because they weren't properly expressed. Either the sacred container I talked about was never created, or it was too small and shattered because it wasn't big enough for both partners to grow. The other scenario is that neither partner expresses their needs and the couple simply grows apart. Either way, infidelity is brutal and I hope that through personal development it can be avoided.

Some say "Once a partner is unfaithful, can the relationship be restored? Can all be forgiven?" What do you think? Let's look at it together through the first ideal of the Father Wake Rider.

Rider Reminders

- Integrating all of the ideals of the Son and Warrior will help you become the ultimate Lover.
- Platonic intimacy is a state you can reach with a close friend when you trust each other enough to be vulnerable because each of you value each other's worth.
- Consent applies to all relationships, not just sexual ones.

Lover Section Takeaways

The Third B Word—Being

The word *being* helps the Lover Wake Rider remember to stay in sync to experience ideal states. How are you being? Are you showing others acts of kindness or are you stuck in a victim mentality thinking the world has done you wrong? Are you being authentic and open with your loved ones? Are you expressing your emotions or keeping them bottled up?

Life is not really about having enough time; it's more about what we want to focus on and apply energy toward, moment by moment.

Loving yourself may look like giving yourself time for rest, reflection, and 100% not feel guilty for doing so.

Being available to other people is at the foundation of the Lover, but if you don't want to make yourself available to others, this is about self-love, too. If someone is projecting onto you negative thoughts or energy, ask yourself how available you want to be to their behavior. Do you want to believe them? Do you want them to knock you off your wake or mess up your ride?

People can influence how we feel only if we let them. Others can hinder our movement toward an aspiration. We can choose to be available to let them do this—Or we can choose not to engage.

Working with energy is about being available to the Spirit. God's love shows up in so many ways. We are given ideas to help us solve problems. We're given beauty to enjoy, whether it's music, the sky, nature, artwork, food, and whatever else we can enjoy or admire.

Rite of Passage

Even though we can have exquisite physical experiences with a lover it may take countless experiments with different lovers to find the sacred ground. There is a lot of confusion in society about love and unfortunately, a lot of men don't get to experience the nirvana of a sacred partnership. Processing the hurt he experiences due to broken relationships is the Lover's Rite of Passage. One thing related to this has to do with the loneliness and pain of not reaching the invulnerable sacred stage with another person. This pain is what transitions the Lover Wake Rider into the next phase of development—the Father.

Exercise

Make a list of the characteristics of your ideal Lover. Include everything—their physical looks, their temperament, what they are into, etc. If you have a lover, share your list and what you love about them. Also, make a list of at least twenty things you love about yourself and share this, too.

PART FOUR - The Father

The Father Wake Rider
One to Many

"Is there anything worse than blindness? Oh yes! Having sight but no vision." —Helen Keller [16]

Introducing the Father

One may make the obvious assumption that the Father Wake Rider is the result of a man and a woman getting together and having children. But the truth is that you don't need to have your own kids to be a father figure. You will encounter tons of scenarios where you influence others whether you are the boss at work, a volunteer at your church or that go-to uncle for your sister's kids.

I hypothesize that there is a lot of suffering in the world because many people don't have father figures in their life. This can show up three different ways. One scenario is that your biological father simply isn't in your life. Mom may have raised you on her own because your dad flew the coop. Another scenario is when your dad is physically in your life but is so caught up on being the financial provider for your family that he's missing because he's at work a lot. And when that little version of you asked him to play catch or go to your baseball game he was exhausted, or too stressed to really engage with you. The third scenario is when Dad is emotionally unavailable because *he* is still broken and has too many wounds that he is dealing with.

This section is important because it is the summation of the other Wake Riders, all coming together into one. The other Wake Riders are still a part of who we are, but the Father is the actualized person who has experienced the Rite of Passages the other three needed to experience in order to feel completely whole.

The Father Wake Rider is about what's beyond the traumas and tests the previous versions of ourselves went through. We have scar tissue built up, but we can see what's on the other side of all the hurts. We let go of transgressions quicker and act with more mercy. We can now find peace.

In chapter twelve, I talked about how the Lover starts to understand how everything is sacred. He learns about having sacred exchanges with others and there is reverence that can be expressed towards all living things. This is the beginning stage of the Father as he realizes there is an entire world beyond his physicality.

Whether we achieve a sacred love partnership or not, it is at this stage of our development where we can start to feel invulnerable. In my opinion, I feel enlightenment is when we realize the need for protection and safety is something of a myth. You now know that all of the scary potential scenarios you made up in your head hardly ever actually happen. You now have evidence that what plays out in reality is never as bad as what was in your head. When you start feeling invulnerable, you can finally get to the point where you ask yourself, "What was it I needed protection from?"

The Father Wake Rider knows just because you can't see something doesn't mean it doesn't exist, and he has the ability to tap into this unseen source of intelligence. Being in touch with his wise, old soul, the Father provides wisdom to his tribe.

Because he has learned how to manage his fears, he begins living with a sense of purpose.

The Father's Desire

What is left for the Father to desire? I've covered ecstasy, the desire to be accepted, and to win. What's left? A while ago I got my answer and it's probably one of the main reasons I'm writing this book. In fact, I understood the Father's root desire before I understood the others.

I've spent a good portion of my life not believing in myself. I wasted a lot of emotional energy wishing others believed in me. This was a big distortion in my marriage. During the "honeymoon" phase, my newlywed wife saw a lot of potential in me. I was pretty confident at first, but it sort of wore off as time went by. I distinctly remember thinking to myself, "If Deb just believed in me, then I could succeed." Sadly, it turned into a self-fulfilling prophecy. The more I wanted people to believe in me, the weaker I appeared. I think this ties in to a lot of faulty habits fathers have like the need to be right, the judging, the moral superiority complex, always having something to prove, the anxiety over worrying about how your life appears, and the list goes on. Sadly, I experienced a lot of this in my marriage.

A couple of years ago, I was doing some soul searching (as usual) and I was thinking about my kids and my relationship with them. I was also realizing how important it was to believe I had what it took to achieve my dreams and experience my life the way I wanted to live it. Then I got an urge to text this message to my oldest daughter:

Do you believe in me?

She wrote me a message about how lucky she felt to have me as her Dad and how proud of me she was and that, *of course,* she believes in me.

Reading that message, I had the most amazing feeling. Those few sentences filled me up inside and any worries or doubts I had about my life disappeared. This dialog stayed with me and it's kept me moving forward in many areas of my life. It was such a profound feeling and is hard to explain, but there is something to this, and it resonates at the core of who I am as a father.

There is something very powerful behind the idea of a father's children having confidence in him and it's even sweeter when the kids are adults. The root desire of the Father Wake Rider is to be believed. The reason this is true is because if he's teaching people and they believe him, his memories and thoughts live on. It's proof that he lived. He was here. He was alive. Think of the spelling of *believe* and how it resembles BE LIVE.

Another way of looking at wanting to be believed is the idea of being an influencer. And like the other Wake Rider root desires in and of itself being an influence isn't bad. It's when we get consumed by it that it can cause distortions. I spoke in the Lover section about social media. I feel that people are obsessed with trying to influence others with their posts. It is over the top and the platforms feed off of this. In a wholesome sense, if you have credible and educational information to share that is fine, but when you go to such an extreme that you have anxiety over how many comments and likes you get, this desire to influence can be unhealthy in my opinion.

Paradoxically, this is something I personally am struggling with because I want my ideas to get out there for people to consider and I know most likely that building communities and groups on social media platforms will be one of the most effective ways of doing this.

Why This is Important

There are two very big reasons why it's important to heal fathers. The first reason is quite shocking and not many people think about it. When I was working on the second round of revisions of this book, I was having a big *why me* episode going on. Experts call this *imposter syndrome* and it describes how authors and coaches begin questioning if they're good enough to put their message out to the masses.

I had a pretty bad case of imposter syndrome until I heard some profoundly sad news from one of my friends. She was upset because her stepmom's father committed suicide at the age of 84. She felt that he did this because he didn't want to be too much of a burden on the family after they decided to take him in versus putting him in a nursing home.

This was gut-wrenchingly sad news for me. I thought about how low he must've been to take his own life. That got me over the imposter syndrome real fast because I figured that if one person reads this book and doesn't commit suicide as a result of something I wrote, then the effort to write this book would be worth it.

Shortly after this tragedy, I learned some startling facts published by the CDC referencing the National Violent Death Reporting System. In 2019 there were over 47,511 suicides and 1.38 million attempts. The number one demographic who committed suicide was men between the ages of 40-65+.

This really struck me because of all the kids who are left without a father or grandfather. Suicide is already very sad, regardless of the demographic. But this statistic really weighed on my heart because I'm in this age bracket and I understand some of the despair men my age experience.

The second reason it is important to heal fathers is because it's time to break the cycle of men not being available to their family. Frankly, it's time to stop the breeding of asshole dads who perpetuate bad parenting.

Women talk about breaking the cycle of abuse. They hit a point where they aren't going to allow the abuse anymore. They want to move out and create a new life for themselves and their children. They have a new set of standards they want to establish for themselves and their kids. And when they succeed at moving out, the cycle of abuse ends.

The bad dad cycle needs to end. When we are great fathers, we are molding a new generation of great men and exemplifying a high standard for our daughters too. The topic of healing the father is important because there doesn't seem to be very many great examples of excellent fathers anymore in the public eye.

I'm not 100% clear why it seems like there aren't a lot of great role models for young men. Maybe it is because we have so much access to the media and we are bombarded by stories of men being caught in scandalous behavior. Or maybe we are so competitive and get so busy comparing ourselves to others that we get addicted to drama and we even seem to take pleasure in seeing heroes fall.

The purpose of this section of the book is to begin sharing thoughts about what I think the byproducts look like that healed fathers begin to experience. Some of these ideas may be a bit lofty, too deep, far fetched, and even controversial, but the goal is to begin painting the picture of what a man looks like who has expanded his awareness and has worked on becoming the best version of himself.

Who Comes to Mind When I Think of the Father Wake Rider

If we go back to the idea of an immature and a mature version of the Wake Rider, two examples come to mind. The character Steve Martin plays in *Father of the Bride* is what reminds me of an immature father. He is full of love. He wants to give advice and be relevant. He also sees his kids growing up and moving on with their lives. He experiences sadness over all of this. He still has plenty of insecurities he's dealing with, but he embodies some of the Father Wake Rider ideals such as the desire to be a good teacher to his kids and being a forgiving person.

Who reminds me of the mature version of the Father? I think our Creator is the ultimate example of the Father Wake Rider. It would be easy to get caught in a trap here, and this may turn off a few people regarding the gender of God, and other religious dogma, but in my opinion, God transcends gender and represents everything beyond our physical reality. The mature Father Wake Rider understands concepts such as eternity, abundance, mercy, and infinity. I feel a mature father is in touch with his soul and when he feels healed and whole those ideals show up on a regular basis.

Core Strength of the Father

The word that comes to mind for the Father's core strength is *Encore*. This is when an audience demands that a performer give something extra beyond the original show.

I like to think mature Fathers have this ability. They always have a little something extra inside of them to give when called upon. They always know the next thing. If a son asks his father for advice, the mature Father can share something beyond what the son is expecting. The Father Wake Rider asks the next question and always knows what's up ahead. This is a core strength of the Father that is rarely talked about.

I saw this in my own dad when he was dying from cancer. I never saw him break down or freak out. He just kept moving ahead with dignity. He completed all the radiation therapy and put himself through a ton of pain because of the love he had for my Mom. He prepared ahead of time for all the things my Mom would need when he was gone. He made sure all of his investments were in order, he bought a new car six months before he passed knowing my Mom would need a reliable vehicle. He even had all his funeral details worked out ahead of time. He was prepared for what was to come after his performance, just like an actor is prepared to give an encore.

Amazon Therapy

I realized when I truly started to feel whole was when I was struggling financially at the time I was delivering packages for Amazon. I call this story *Amazon Therapy*, but could just as easily call it *Driving in the Shadows*. In her book *Dark Side of Light Chasers*, Debbie Ford tells us in order to be truly healed we need to be able to accept and see the gifts in our darker emotions, and until we do this we can't totally heal. During this phase of my life, I was processing an assortment of issues centered around fear, shame, judging, and anger.

I mentioned in chapter five that I had a fear around running out of money. One thing that helped me get a handle on this was a phone app a friend told me about called *Amazon Flex*. Anyone can download the app and create an income by doing deliveries for Amazon if there is a distribution center near them. It's like Uber for boxes, but you don't have to deal with drunk people barfing in your car.

As a self-employed content producer, there's a lot of expectations to meet and a lot of pressure to perform. By contrast, what I liked about *Amazon Flex* was how little brain power it required. I could literally go to the warehouse, load a bunch of boxes in my car and the app would tell me precisely where to go. It was this no-brainer, no-pressure situation, and money got deposited into my bank every Tuesday and Friday. I figured on the days I did Amazon. I could just stay up late and do my *real* work for clients later at night.

When you go to the warehouse to pick up your packages you don't know what area you are going to deliver to until you get your rack of boxes. It occurred to me one time I might have to deliver to some not-so-great neighborhoods

One such occasion happened when I had a route for South St. Louis City and East St. Louis. I don't know if you saw *National Lampoon's Vacation* with Chevy Chase where he's driving around St. Louis by the Arch and gets off track and he misses a turn, and somehow ends up in East St. Louis. Well, the movie is not too unrealistic...I mean, there are areas over there that kind of look like Beirut. I decided to reverse my route and start my deliveries in East St. Louis during the day and then finish in South City in the evening.

When I was delivering packages in East St. Louis, I was really observing what the surroundings were like in the daylight. There were heavily industrialized areas with funny smells spewing out of factories and a lot of railroad tracks. As a matter of fact, I got stopped by a couple of trains and had to halt my deliveries as I waited for the trains to go by. It felt like a mystical experience where something was controlling me and my time, and I started to become hyper-aware of everything. This might have had to do with some sort of fight or flight reflex, but my senses told me I needed to pay extra attention. So, my *alertness level* was definitely kicking in.

As I was driving around, I became very aware of all the contrasts. There was gentrification in some areas, industrial sites, and residential neighborhoods where there were new homes on one street, and boarded-up houses just a block away. It was fascinating to see how many different things were going on. I made it a point to take my time and observe.

Normally when I do deliveries, I'm in a hurry to get done so I can make the most money possible per hour. I usually just run to the front door, put the package on the porch, ring the doorbell, and not wait for the door to be answered. You take a picture of the package on the porch to prove you delivered it, and then you run to your car and you're off to the next stop.

On this particular day, I was really intentional and careful to make sure somebody was home to accept the delivery. I'd stop, ring the doorbell, and wait to hand-deliver the package to the person. I was deliberate for a couple of reasons. The first reason is because you get penalized by Amazon if your packages don't get delivered. If you're in an area where there's a problem with theft you still get penalized. It's not a monetary penalty, but they keep track of the percentage of packages that go missing. If you have a lot of packages not showing up, you can get deactivated.

The second reason I was so deliberate was because I wanted them to see *my light* and my acceptance of them as if to say here's this guy just standing there with their package wishing them a happy day. One byproduct of doing this Amazon gig is that it gives you the opportunity to make thousands of people happy. People love it when their stuff arrives, and it's kind of cool being the person who makes them happy. (Kinda like Santa Claus – now there's a Whole Dude!)

We all feel the fun and joy when a package is delivered to us. After I handed them their package, I told them each "Have a good one" very casually. I'd like to think I was shifting the energy a little by putting off positive vibes non-verbally, hopefully diminishing just a little bit of the discord in the world by my positive energy.

The other thing I noticed was a subtle yet profound shift in my judging and discerning. I learned a cool little trick to do when I felt judging impulses popping up inside of me. I had this teeny tiny shift in my awareness as my thoughts and feelings moved to fascination instead of judgment.

For example, when I was standing on someone's front porch who had a car up on blocks and next to a boarded up house, in the past I may have thought "What the hell am I doing here?" I suspect these judging feelings are natural reactions for most people. But then I had this shift, and I began being fascinated by *everything!* I began to ask questions like "Why is this neighborhood like this and the other neighborhood a block away is brand new?" and "I wonder if there's a lot of political corruption which causes this to persist?" I became fascinated wondering "Who lives in this house? What will they look like when they answer the door?"

There is a more expansive *fascination* energy that shows up for me instead of judging when these situations happen now. This fascination feeling takes the same amount of effort as judging, but the focus is shifted to a sense of wonderment. Like what I talked about in the "Son" section.

I realized that when we're judging others, what we're really doing is judging ourselves. It dawned on me that I was judging myself for delivering for Amazon. After that, I kind of stopped worrying about how much I was making hourly and how efficient I was being. I began to realize I was just creating cash flow and getting things moving financially. Little did I know at the time I'd have more philosophical breakthroughs while making deliveries.

I took a break from doing *Amazon Flex* because things in my main business picked up again due to a large project I had landed. But this changed with the COVID-19 situation and I found I needed to take advantage of my side hustle again. In a lot of ways, I'm glad I did because I evidently needed to do more shadow work (but the money helped, too). I've talked about shame and how it is buried in our psyche and can control us. When I wasn't in the best state of mind, I'd tell myself "Look at you, all your friends are set in their careers making six-figure incomes, and you're driving around hell's acres delivering packages." So yeah, this stuff goes through my head from time to time. However, once I broke through and understood some childhood issues, many of the other things I was ashamed of all seemed to lose their sting and intensity.

I was starting to mellow out quite a bit during this phase of my life. I was witnessing gorgeous scenery when I went on routes in rural areas. I saw countless farmers' fields with row after row of corn. I've witnessed amazing sunsets and gorgeous fields of sunflowers. It was fun sometimes pretending I was a Le Mans race car driver going around windy roads. One day I might be delivering in neighborhoods where every house is over a million dollars, and the next day I'd be in an area where everyone is living in a mobile home in a trailer park. It's really quite fascinating to see the variety of lifestyles and the contrasts and not judge either way of being.

One Saturday I had plans to have dinner with my Mom and was going to go straight to her house after my route. That day, for whatever reason, my route was flat-out ridiculous. It was way longer than it should have been. Amazon uses some sort of algorithm to put together routes, and gives a pretty good estimate on how long it is going to take when they make the offer in the app. The estimates have really gotten more and more accurate, but every once in a while, you get a real booger.

One mishap after another happened that day and I started getting really aggravated. Eventually I became pissed the later it got. I really wanted to get to my Mom's at a decent time and I was getting agitated. Then I thought: "Is Mom really going to be upset if I'm a half-hour late? I mean come on. Really, that's not the issue." Then I wondered if I was mad because somehow Amazon was screwing me. Then I thought about it and figured this was obviously not the case. I came to grips with the fact that Amazon is just being Amazon.

Then I thought some more and the answer came to me... "I'm angry because I'm disappointed in myself. I'm disappointed in my financial situation. I'm disappointed that it's Saturday and all my friends are probably out enjoying their families or partying and here I am delivering packages to Villa "fucking" Ridge Missouri—WTF!" I sat with this anger a while and reflected a little bit on the circumstances I had gotten myself into. Then, slowly but surely, I started being okay. I started to forgive myself. This was a *huge* breakthrough for me.

I got to see my mind literally manipulate me to get angry, and then I got to see a gentle release and acceptance. I got to see that my anger is 100% under my control. I saw how I could feel the rage and process it. I realized no matter what situation I'm in, I can handle the anger and not let it take over me. And even *if* I get really upset, it has a purpose. I got to see how I worked through the negative emotions and overcome them in a pretty short amount of time. I realized as long as I didn't lash out or harm anyone, this was a natural process that helped release past traumas and to witness parts of me that needed to still be heard and healed. To experience how all this unfolded that day felt incredible.

About a week later, I was driving out in the middle of nowhere again and was really admiring the countryside. I said to myself, "Look at this, I get to get paid to go on a spectacular Sunday drive." Then I realized I could adopt this way of thinking in all areas of my life. I started observing my thoughts during my drive and had quite a few laughs.

I had a shift from thoughts of *I have to,* to, *I get to.* I composed a mental list as I drove through the woods and thought:

- I get to become really good at figuring out North, South, East, and West on cloudy days.
- I get to learn about how fast 250 feet comes up when you're going 40 miles an hour.
- I get to get really good at reading upside down.
- I get to get really good at driving in reverse down long skinny driveways.
- I get to discover exquisite neighborhoods in St. Louis I didn't know existed and study all the amazing architecture.
- I get to get paid to do wind sprints every 3-4 minutes.

That Amazon gig didn't make me a lot of money and was a very short episode of my life. But it was priceless in the ways it helped me evolve into a more peaceful person and played a role in me seeing the sacredness of everything.

I share these stories because I believe they really relate to one's transcendence to the Father Wake Rider and how his perspective encourages joy, acceptance, humility, and peace.

These are examples of how I grew and learned how to handle anger, fear, my ego and how I became less judgemental. The main message I want to share about being a father is that at some point if we are able to heal aspects of ourselves we can become like the Father Wake Rider who develops the capacity to have mercy and be less reactionary to situations that happen to him. Prior to this development he may become unhinged when he encounters these types of situations.

Chapter Thirteen—I'm Done Hurting Myself

"How unhappy is he who cannot forgive himself." —Publilius Syrus [17]

Father Ideal Number One—Forgiving

People give lip service to the concept of forgiveness when they say things like, "I will forgive, but I'll never forget" as if they deserve a badge of honor for this behavior. It seems like a waste of energy to cling onto hurt feelings in my opinion. I guess that is okay to feel that way, but I think sometimes people use this to try to one up each other. Like people say "misery loves company." I think some people actually kind of get some sort of affirmation of their worth or something when they emote the feeling of "yeah I see you're hurt, but you're not as hurt as me." It's sort of like the scene in Jaws when the character played by Richard Dreyfuss is comparing all of his scars with the captain of the boat.

The good news is that some people are now realizing if they hold onto grudges, they're really hurting themselves. In addition to not holding onto grudges, I'm starting to see how everything mirrors back to me revealing what I need to learn. I've begun analyzing my reactions to triggers and now I can recognize old patterns and what they mean. Sometimes I can figure out the buried message from the pain pretty quickly. I've learned that I can have personal development breakthroughs almost instantly when the lesson from the shadow is accepted.

Sadly, some things may take me years and years and years to figure out.

I've had a recent situation where I forgave my ex-girlfriend's ex-husband for being a jerk to her and me. It took me three years, but I realized he was just unintentionally mirroring back behaviors I didn't like about myself. The key to forgiving him was how I learned the lesson the triggers were trying to teach me. The funny thing is that I hadn't even thought of the guy in three years, but there obviously must have been a shadow within me needing to surface and heal. Was he a narcissistic jerk? Probably, but in the moment I had the choice of how to react to his behavior and not get tweaked by his actions.

What I Used to Do

I've been a little bit rough on my Dad throughout this book. While he was strict, often irritable, and had a pretty bad temper, he wasn't an absolute monster! One of the byproducts of growing up with a strict and stern Dad was the need to avoid his wrath. I was a very meek person who didn't want to rock the boat. Having an overly stressed household was not always the case, though.

When we lived in the city, I think our family was a lot more easygoing and playful. Even though I was a really young kid, I remember playing with our neighbors, the Brothertons, who went to our church and also had seven kids in their family. At any given moment there could be the chaos of 10–14 kids playing in the house.

I remember a Union Electric Christmas Party and driving out to the UE Country Club in West County in my Dad's green 1970 Ford Torino station wagon and laying in the back feeling the heat come off of the wheel well while falling asleep to the reverberation of the music coming out of my Dad's groovy quadraphonic stereo on the way home. I felt safe. I didn't even know what conflict was back then. Those were the days of my innocence when I thought my Dad could do no wrong.

But something shifted when we moved out of the city to West St. Louis County. My Dad seemed to get much more uptight and grumpier. He had to do shift work and had very weird schedules and sleeping patterns and as a result this had a big impact on my upbringing. I mention this because I think a common concern a lot of guys have is that they don't want to turn into their old man. This is a very real issue for a lot of us, and I can honestly say one of the reasons I married Debbie was because I indeed didn't want to turn into my Dad when I got older and knew she would never allow it.

The other thing worth noting here is the forgiveness process I went through. I would not be exaggerating if I said my Dad emotionally and verbally abused me and my siblings. He could be pretty damn scary at times. I also believe he probably had no idea the impact his behavior was having on his kids, or at least not until the damage was done. I've heard stories from my Mom about how they'd lay in bed at night and he would beat himself up because he didn't think he was a very good dad.

I had to let go of all that pain and move on. If I was going to have any shot at self-love and self-worth, I had to try to put myself in his shoes and accept him. I tell people sometimes, "Holy crap, I'd be the same as him if I was in that situation, I mean, come on, how stressful would it be to raise *seven* kids?" He *had* to crack the whip and run a tight ship, or the inmates would have taken over the asylum! Unfortunately, I don't think many people are capable of fully letting go of childhood pain or emotional trauma without help.

But the thing is, my Dad started to mellow out as he got older, and I consider myself lucky to have seen a softer side of him. I'm glad I *did the work* and forgave him, and thus it allowed me to melt the walls between us and have closure when he passed away. What also helped me tremendously was that I realized the gifts I received from my upbringing. I realized that because of my experiences and environment as a kid, I began to develop the ability to sense people's energy. Often on my way home from school as I walked down my street, I could start feeling the domineering energy of my Dad's presence and I knew that I should go straight to my room and not be noticed. Other times I sensed things were okay before I got home and knew that I could play and everything would be fine. I think this precognitive sense is a quality that comes in handy as an adult and really helps me in my interactions with people.

So Dad, if you're seeing this from Heaven, I love you and I'm thankful for all you taught me.

What I Do Now

How do we forgive people? I do not want to just regurgitate all the common axioms that exist around the topic of forgiveness in general because there is plenty of material out there already to consume. I do want to share some personal insights based on what I'm learning from studying *A Course in Miracles*.

According to their website, *A Course in Miracles* is a self-study spiritual thought system. ACIM teaches that the way to universal love and peace—or remembering God—is by undoing guilt through forgiving others. The Course thus focuses on the healing of relationships and making them holy.

My biggest breakthrough from *ACIM* is how I now realize *I'm* the person hurting myself with my thoughts. ACIM calls these *attack* thoughts and I am the one who originates these thoughts. We are hardwired to assign meaning to our experiences, and this includes what people say. I choose if I am going to let what I hear make me feel bad. Sometimes people say things not intended to be hurtful, yet we unconsciously take it as an attack. I used to drive Deb crazy when I'd constantly read between the lines of everything she'd say. I told myself recently, "I'm done hurting myself and I'm done causing anxiety based on my definition of what I apply to circumstances." I seriously think this is the ultimate version of self-love, too. After I had this epiphany, I can honestly say I don't get upset with people as often, and when I do the sting or bitterness doesn't last very long. I can now let go of hurt feelings pretty easily.

Another thing that has helped me is realizing *perceptions are not* reality. People say "perception is reality" but I claim it isn't. My viewpoint is pretty contrary to conventional thinking. I feel people get too attached to what they perceive as being real. I believe everyone perceives things differently and these perceptions are very real to them. For instance, we have heard about cases where people are interviewed at a crime scene, and everyone has a different recollection of what happened. This is because everyone's vantage point of the scene is different. Also, people's biases can come into play to complicate situations even more. Therefore, how can perception be reality if everyone has a different perspective? Saying "Perception is *not* reality" makes it easier for me to be more forgiving. It basically gives the other person an automatic hall pass. If my perceptions can be wrong, so can theirs, and vice versa.

Ultimately it boils down to us forgiving ourselves for having a wrong perception and for believing an illusion. If we can get to this degree of personal development our life can be full of grace, ease, and a whole new level of acceptance.

Getting to this place may not happen overnight, but one thing I've realized is whenever these *bad things* happen, there is an opportunity to learn and evolve. When a feeling of hurt wells up inside of me because of an undesirable situation, I've recently begun asking: "What am I learning about myself from this situation?" This changes the focus and quickly derails any bitter feelings from getting out of control.

Often the easiest way to forgive is to just realize all people have their own issues they're dealing with. Also, they may not even realize they've done anything harmful to you because they are so caught up in their own head. So, if you can try to see things from their perspective, this will reduce the intensity of the situation a bit and diffuse some of the hard feelings.

The Father Wake Rider ultimately mimics God's ability to forgive everyone. I mean, think about it—how many billions of people are living on Earth? Seven billion people are doing bad things individually and collectively, and God continues to forgive us! If we can learn to have mercy and forgive others and ourselves, I think we can rapidly improve the quality of our life.

And finally, forgiveness work is integrating acceptance and accountability. What this might look like is to admit it takes two to tango. There could be a very good explanation why someone gets mad and lashes out at us in the first place. We may have actually done something to contribute to the situation. Consider playing back the scenario and seeing what your role was. Owning your behavior and acknowledging what you did can speed up the forgiveness process and the healing between everyone involved.

Father Distortion Number One—Too Hurt

Like so many of these ideals, forgiveness has a couple of extreme variations. A passive distortion of forgiveness is when we get stuck and we're not able to forgive somebody or a circumstance in our life because we are just too hurt.

We can have an event occur which takes us an entire lifetime to forgive. We have all heard about families where siblings end up never communicating ever again because of deep-seated resentments. I feel like when we are in situations like this, we are surrendering potential joy if we insist on staying hurt.

We have free will and we can choose to stay disconnected and unforgiving. Sometimes, we're intentionally choosing to stay in a state of victimhood. These situations can be so dastardly we get stuck and cannot see the lesson.

Here's the deal: I don't want to sound too holier-than-thou here and I want to keep it real. Many of us have had trauma in our life, which takes a long, long time to process and heal. We have scar tissue from past trauma and it can be tender even after years have passed. It might seem impossible to let whoever caused the hurt off the hook, let alone have compassion for them. I get this and want to honor where many of you may be in terms of being too hurt still to forgive. My intent is to simply share some of my experiences so they might act as a reference and hopefully share a new perspective that might help you heal. I don't want to do a bypass though acting like this is as easy as doing some meditation which magically causes all the hurt to evaporate.

I talk to people about the divine perfection in everything. If we can stretch a little, we can realize there might even be perfection in these hurtful situations. If you keep asking questions and continue learning, you may realize that this process is part of our healing. Somehow, this molds us into who we are becoming as a person.

A friend of mine who exemplifies all of this is my *ACIM* course facilitator, Connie. Her son was innocently killed as the result of a police car chase. No parent on earth deserves to go through the pain of losing a child or the ongoing process of seeking justice for that child. The grief she's graciously working through is profound. Honestly, I'm not able to relate to this degree of pain because nothing so devastating has happened to me.

I think how she's moving towards forgiveness is by finding the purpose in the pain. With unshakeable faith in God having a plan for her, she's been learning a lot about overcoming emotional pain and understanding how her grieving process could potentially help others who are experiencing grief. What makes Connie amazing is how she keeps things completely real. When she's hurting, she admits it, and feels it, and doesn't just sweep things under the rug. Many people in similar pain act like things are *fine* when they don't want to let anyone in.

I'm not pretending to portray that I'm able to overcome the majority of hurtful events anyone faces in life, but I do feel like I have been through a bit of sorrow myself. In my personal situation, I would have to say my *work* on this topic is related to my youngest daughter, Alli.

She's a unique child with learning delays and was diagnosed at a young age with cerebral palsy. Thankfully, I've been at peace with all of this for a long time and I acknowledge Alli's a great teacher for me and she's a huge reason why I'm the person I am today. I could contemplate the unfairness of the situation. I could compare my life to the numerous friends of mine who have perfectly healthy kids. If I'm truly honest, I have to admit that I probably did have some bitterness over the years. I could have sat there and been depressed comparing my life to friends that have had perfect careers and beautiful paid-off homes, but what's the point?

If I wallow in the supposed unfairness, I'm the one doing the hurting. A few months ago, I had an epiphany during what could have turned into a pity party. Instead of falling into the trap of victimhood thoughts, I decided that, moving forward, I would always tell myself I'm grateful because I get to be the Dad of this very unique child. Alli has an amazing sense of wonder and asks a ton of questions just like a small child even though she's twenty-one years old. This sense of curiosity is just who she is. It's all she knows, and this way of being is her *normal*. She's a constant reminder to me about how important it is to be open to letting everything just be, without judging so quickly. I cannot tell you the number of times she's said "Who cares?" I'm not sure where this attitude came from, but man, it's a pretty damn good way to react to life.

I understand people's suffering to some degree, and why people stay hurt or think God wronged them in some way.

I get it.

There was a time when I didn't know if my daughter was going to walk. I had to have faith she would though, but admittedly it was a pretty scary time in my life. The profound amount of joy I had on vacation in Destin the day she walked unassisted for the first time from couch to couch in the condo was definitely a top ten moment in my life. Up until then, she needed a walker to help her with her balance and she hated it. I thanked God and all the heavenly hosts that Alli was going to be able to walk on her own without assistance. And right after this joyful moment, I had the thought of "okay good, now we can start working full time on trying to get Alli to talk." This sounds awful, but it was what I thought.

Then there was the day when the Head Speech Pathologist at St. Louis University told Debbie and me she thought our child might not speak. I was like "Ah, hell no—that dog don't hunt." Deb and I made it our mission to get Alli to talk. I hope to one day write a book to share her journey and I'd like to call it "*Speechless.*"

The point is to realize there are situations in our life where it's easy to stay stuck in a place of not being able to forgive because we hurt really bad. We can get in a funk and never get out. While Alli still has some issues with her speaking, like not using full sentences and speaking with poor grammar, she *does* talk, and I even have to tell her to shut up sometimes, but I'll take it. We still have some uncertainty around where her career is heading and what type of work she will be able to do, but I have to rest in my belief that everything happens for a reason and in a divine sort of order. All is well.

Father Distortion Number Two—Vengeful

If being too hurt to forgive is the passive extreme of the forgiveness ideal, the aggressive extreme is wanting to exact revenge on those who hurt you. This distortion is about how anger can lead to doing regrettable things.

This comes full circle with the concept of being hurt and the topic of protection. When you're in a mindset of needing revenge, things have definitely been spiraling downward, and the need for vengeance is just the tip of the iceberg of other issues going on. It's the straw that breaks the camel's back.

As the saying goes "Hurt people hurt people."

From a general sense, being angry, resentful, and bitter reminds me of a line in Sting's song *"If I Ever Lose My Faith in You,"* when he says "I never saw no military solution/ That didn't always end up as something worse." People seeking revenge have been going on since the dawn of Man. This mentality breeds a vicious, unbreakable cycle of hate and pain.

What does hate get us? When someone feels like they must get revenge, it seems they are channeling some form of bravery. Also, it seems like society glorifies this mindset. When someone is scheming and planning their revenge, it's like they are some sort of hero *doing the right thing* or *standing up for what is right*. A good example of this is The Count of Monte Cristo – one of the greatest books written about revenge, yet at the end he learns how destructive and hollow it is.

I see how manipulative the movie industry can be and is pervasive in embedding the psychology and teachings of vengeance. Their subtle message is about how important it is to be *a real man* and get back at the other person. They insinuate you are weak and a coward if you don't set things straight. This is sad because it is an influence on young men and confuses people to think this is how we are supposed to be.

Violence and revenge get us *nowhere*.

As a species, our survival depends on us expanding our consciousness and overcoming this savage behavior. We can start personally by looking beyond needing to always be right. We can stop needing to lash out at others because we think they are wrong. We can pause and start not always feeling threatened and needing to pre-empt people out of fear of getting hurt.

Peace and forgiveness are the only sustainable solution. Unfortunately, generation after generation has been hurt and traumatized. While this is coming to the surface right now at the meta-level, this has to do with equality and respect. By knowing we've all been hurt at some point in our life, we can begin to foster an attitude of tolerance and hopefully transform into a less violent world.

One way to distract yourself while you are angry and thinking you need revenge is to ask yourself "Why is this situation showing up and what can I learn on a deeper level?"

Our world is very destructive right now and it's starting to feel like we're going to burn this civilization down and start all over again. I think one of the solutions is to understand our spiritual nature, which is peaceful and not destructive. And to realize we are on earth to love and serve one another.

I don't know the final answer and I don't know if Mankind is going to destroy itself but my intention is to try to provide examples of wholeness to dudes so they can continue on their path of conscious expansion and help with the collective healing of Mankind. I texted a friend of mine: "Healed people heal people." When more people heal, more people *can* heal.

Hurting people is the opposite of love and needing revenge is the opposite of healing. It's not a good place to be emotionally when you feel like you need revenge. When we feel whole, we are feeling love. Wanting to hurt someone for any reason whatsoever is the opposite of being a loving person.

One of my goals is to create a community of men who can be there for each other when we need someone to listen as we process toxic situations in our lives and hopefully, we can find peaceful solutions versus vengeful actions.

Forgiveness is a gateway to our spirituality. While it isn't easy to forgive, we're keeping ourselves disconnected from our Source when we don't. The next chapter talks about spirituality and I try to simplify this often complex topic, I strived to keep my ideas neutral and digestible for everyone.

Rider Reminders

- It can be hard to forgive and that is ok; but if we can it's a gateway to peace and a way to reconnect with our Source.
- Practicing forgiveness is like a muscle that can be developed one situation at a time.
- The need for revenge causes a loop that never ends.

Chapter Fourteen—Look Beyond Religion

"Science is not only compatible with spirituality; it is a profound source of spirituality." —Carl Sagan [18]

Father Ideal Number Two—Spiritual

Here is a very simple and practical way to understand spirituality. Whether you think you are religious or not and even if you don't believe in God, I can assure you that you've witnessed spirituality.

If you've ever been to a football game at your alma mater, you can totally feel the unity and connection you have with everyone on your side of the stands. Someone who otherwise is a complete stranger is standing by you cheering, giving high-fives, and screaming at the refs right along with you. No one is at the game arguing over what name to use for God. You just sense the energy and you feel the connection with everyone on your side. It feels like you are part of something bigger than yourself.

Churches can also have this feeling of unity. The members of a church share common values and the congregation feels like they are part of something bigger than themselves. There is also a concentration of everyone's energy at a church that quantum physics calls a morphic field. You can't see it but it feels good. This smells like team spirit to me!

I feel the urge to belong exists because people sense something is missing in their life. They can't see it with their eyes but they feel it can be filled by being involved with like-minded people.

Community is related to this too. In this modern era, we all yearn to connect and engage with a group of like-minded people. When we have a community with common interests and missions, we feel like we are part of something bigger than ourselves and this can satiate our appetite of having to fulfill a life purpose. Facebook groups and other online communities where people hang out with their tribe seem to be the modern-day replacement for churches and religion. I do believe if this is the path for some people to find their unique version of spirituality, more power to them.

Facebook profiles' asks us about our religious views and I wrote "It's a God thing," which is me basically saying "I don't want to be compartmentalized." In this same sense, I'm going to make a similar suggestion about spirituality. While I think being spiritual is really important, I truly believe people have every right to find their own way to God.

If you can begin to think of spirituality from a perspective of us all connecting, having a common interest, and accepting one another, it gets easier to discover and develop a practice where you can look beyond religion.

What could this be like you may ask? I think instead of dividing the readers of this book, via differing religious beliefs. I'm proposing we take some of the dogma and disagreement out of the topic of spirituality. If we can all agree on a term to describe this, we can then be on the same page. For the sake of this discussion I'm recommending we replace the words God, Shiva, Universe, Allah, Zero Point Field, Life Force Energy, Yahweh, Buddha, Heavenly Father, Durga, or whatever name you give this phenomenon, and just call it LOVE.

Can we agree, right now, that spirituality is ultimately based on an infinite source of love?

Many people see fathers as the spiritual leader of the family. I portray the Father Wake Rider to be an elder in union with Spirit because he can sense this connection when his life is in sync. And this can act as a guidance system he can tap into for infinite wisdom and he can truly become aware of his own soul.

What I Used To Do

I mentioned in the Son Takeaway section that our beliefs are inherited from our parents and usually, this is the case with religion. I took going to church every Sunday pretty seriously and practiced Catholicism up until my daughter Carlye was born in 1996.

A year or so prior to this, Deb and I began choosing a cafeteria-style religious practice. What I mean by this is we were kind of burnt out and were picking and choosing the *rules* that fit our lifestyle. We weren't feeling committed enough to raise our daughter Catholic, but we did consider ourselves Christian. We then started going to a United Methodist Church which seemed more upbeat and fulfilling. Sadly, those feelings varied based on whatever pastor came along. About ten years later Deb eventually stopped going to church, but I was on the audio/visual team and felt like I was obligated to fulfill my duties to the team. You see, up to this point my feeling was that God was this entity outside of myself and that I was just an unworthy individual. I was taught basically that I wasn't supposed to sin and that I needed to earn my way into heaven by my good deeds. That entering into heaven had more to do with my acts. I kept going to church for several more years and felt that by serving on the AV team and being a giving person I was somehow going to get into this far off place called heaven when I died.

Unlike this belief that you basically earn your way into heaven, Methodists planted the seed in my head that we don't necessarily get into heaven from our acts, instead all we needed to was to accept that Jesus died for our sins and we'd get into heaven. By accepting Jesus as our Savior we would be *saved*. Eventually I got rubbed the wrong way because my church insinuated that it was my job to evangelize this concept and that somehow I had an obligation to help *save people* by sharing this good news. When I started feeling this way it caused me to begin questioning everything.

What I Do Now

I began having a more worldly view of religion. I began learning a lot about other cultures and other saviors. I also started to see the inner play of quantum physics and spirituality.

There are three points I'd like to make in this section of the book:
- I'd love it if people would be more tolerant of other people's religious beliefs. Please take time and *learn*. Language is the main barrier here. If you translate and understand other religions' prayers, you may just find they are very beautiful and can make you more devotional in your own practice.
- The second point to make is that I feel God isn't just this being that is *out there,* but is all around us. My spiritual beliefs eventually grew into being able to feel I'm connected to God. And when I am in a very creative mindset, I can even see how I'm actively co-creating with God. What I mean by this is that I feel like when I am designing things and dreaming up ideas, I realize they are not my own. I feel like what I'm doing is just connecting to thoughts God has already had. Tapping into this, by the way, is something everyone can do because we are all connected. My point about co-creating with God is that I am just dialing in my focus onto something in the aether already and I get to be the one that incubates it and births it into the physical world.
- The third point is this: as important as all this is, there is a lot of mystery and controversy surrounding spirituality. Sadly, when I encounter uber religious people, I get a little twinge of discomfort in my gut due to their convictions and commitment to their version of the truth. I don't want to sound too disrespectful of religious people, but I think it is important to be open minded and to continue to learn and challenge our belief systems. In reality what is it that we really know? We all have unique perspectives, experiences, biases, and beliefs but is any of it the absolute truth?

To expound upon this *not knowing* sentiment and to evoke some pondering, here is a slight tongue-in-cheek list of questions that came to mind about the confusion related to spirituality and philosophy in general:

- Does being spiritual mean I'm better than you?
- Did going to church for over 40+ years of my life count for something?
- Do you arrive at a place of enlightenment and actually know the truth?
- Does the learning end?
- Did Adam ever wake up?
- Is there purpose in the pain or is the pain there just for pain's sake?
- Am I going to Hell because some of my views about Jesus have changed over the last eighteen years?
- Are there really 108 Hindu Gods?
- If CERN splits an atom, will we really learn anything about the Big Bang Theory and the creation story?
- If I recite a mantra singing to Kali Ma does it make me a dark person and if I believe the Ganesh Mantra can really help me get to an appointment on time, would my Christian friends believe me or would they think I'm going to Hell?
- How exactly does the Holy Spirit fit into the equation?
- How does voodoo work?
- Is there life on other planets?
- Does my Dad really pick out songs for me from Heaven when I hit shuffle on my playlist?
- Was that a fox in the middle of the road who looked right at me and then disappeared, and if so, was it some sort of omen, and can Google or Siri *really* explain what it means?
- Did I just do a spiritual bypass?

If you have answers to any of these questions, have questions of your own, or have ideas about being spiritual you want to share please visit:

https://thewholedude.com/spirit

The intent of this chapter is to invite people to take an interest in spirituality. I don't want to be too edgy, compative, or self-righteous either. We may or may not be able to agree on any of it but we can't deny that we feel something. We can't see it, but we are part of something bigger than ourselves.

I personally want to believe my life here on earth has a purpose. I want to honor and admire the grace and beauty of all things. I want to be able to embrace lightness and not fear the darkness it lights up. I want to truly have faith I'm going to be okay.

I recently posted a question on Facebook that asked, "What is the difference between faith and trust? The concept of faith and trust seem to be very similar. It was interesting to see the various replies and this exercise illustrated how people can be very opinionated on topics. The answers varied quite a bit, with most of the responses centered around religion and morality. I think of faith and trust in more general terms.

After I contemplated this question I came up with this: We all want to have faith that we'll be okay. Trust is when we *want* to have faith in something (God, a lover, a vendor, our kids) but we still need some sort of proof. Some people say trust needs to be earned and some people say they trust people until the person breaches their trust.

Faith, to me, is when you *know* everything is well and will work out and you don't need any proof. Spirituality is about this unknown, unseen source we can put our faith in. And when we let go of needing proof, we can experience some real magic. Perhaps the ultimate truth is that the only reason we are here is to learn how to have faith.

Father Distortion Number Three—Too Materialistic

Many traditional religions talk about being meek, not being greedy, not coveting or having your world revolve around *want want want want* so I'd like to give my opinion on this topic. For those of you into the Ten Commandments, you may or may not realize that coveting is the result of a scarcity mindset. Some people think there is only a finite amount of things. In my opinion, coveting is a sin because you're denying that God will provide for you and therefore you want what your neighbor has. We're not really given a deep explanation at Sunday school but we're told not to want other people's stuff.

Ultimately this distorted state is probably going to lead to self-inflicted hurt.

The idea of being too materialistic is a tricky topic. I personally believe God wants us to live an abundant, joyful, epic life. We came to earth to have a human experience and that includes enjoying the things *of the world*.

Many people have figured out there is a lot of truth to the saying "We are in the world, but not of the world." This basically means we are spiritual beings having a human experience in a physical world. Having worldly things is fun, but there is more to life than just accumulating *stuff*. One of the beliefs I'm working on is acknowledging we can be spiritual and not necessarily suffer like a peasant; however, we can't bring our SUV and swimming pool with us when we pass away. Getting really attached to stuff like that can be a recipe for future hurt.

I have heard the word *sin* just means you missed the mark. I think when it comes to possessions and collecting *stuff*, **we miss the mark** when it comes to our thoughts related to *receiving* abundance.

We are taught not to be greedy and instead to be giving and humble. I think all of this is very important, but I also think we don't necessarily need to suffer.

The material world is only the *scorecard* we use to see how life is going for us. When you're whole, you have the following factors working together in your life: and these are the physical, mental, emotional, spiritual, environmental, and relational. The only problem is that of those six aspects of our being, physicality is the only one you can see. Because of this, we mistake reality to be only what can be seen.

The other five factors are invisible and really hard to measure. People *miss the mark* because they get obsessed with the scorecard. I love the saying "the map isn't the territory," and I feel this is another way of making my point about focusing too much on the material world.

Similar to the discussion I had about integrity, I think it is important to look at abundance from a non-judging and non-moralistic vantage point.

Remember, when you sit back and judge people who have a lot of materialistic stuff, it is really you who is judging yourself. The jealousy you have towards others may be caused by the illusion of thinking you need things outside of yourself to make you happy. When things aren't perfect in the outside world, we get agitated, to say the least. The real gold here is when we can be satisfied and very happy without needing to own a lot of material things. We can finally realize love and true happiness are inside jobs.

The other big misstep here is when you compare yourself and circumstances to others. Doing this is the quickest way to get depressed. You drive down the road and you see the guy in the Escalade with the blades (or whatever they call the fancy wheels) and the hot wife with all the bling-bling-bling, and you get envious or judgmental. It is easy to sit there and judge whether you are religious or not. It's like we are allergic to people being superficial, and we equilibrate all the fancy shiny stuff as fake or shallow.

A while ago I had to get real with this part of myself. When I felt those types of feelings I had to sit back and say, "What is it about those people being mirrored back to me that I'm having issues with myself about?" I had an epiphany and figured out I needed to stop judging. I made up my mind that I was happy for those people. They are obviously doing something in their life that is allowing them to be able to afford fancy things.

It then occurred to me what was being reflected back to me was their ability to be good stewards of their money and that I needed to work on that myself. I realized it is a reminder that I have the potential of having abundant finances too if I apply myself. The funny thing now is that *every time* I see a Mercedes it reminds me of abundance in general. I'll probably never buy a Mercedes, by the way.

The other thing about wanting, coveting, and putting our focus solely on the material world is that it literally can cause suffering. I'm seriously going through this right now. I'm tired of just getting by to be perfectly honest. My point is that if we go through life just wanting more and more, or newer and bigger things, it can hurt when it doesn't happen. We can start to question our worthiness and abilities and this is depressing. Having regrets is a big struggle many men have in their later years.

I feel religions are subtly trying to teach us not to be greedy because in the long run we can avoid the suffering caused by the letdown we have when things don't materialize the way we plan.

What I Did Before

I grew up in an affluent area in St. Louis, and became very aware of the existence of class envy at a young age. Sadly, it fostered the ideas of separation and inequality. I learned the difference between the *haves* and the *have nots.* The idea itself is not spiritual at all and is ridiculous because we are all equal.

In retrospect, I can affirm that my family was probably in the *have-not* category. Being one of seven kids growing up in a home controlled by a union Dad who worked shift work for the electric company reinforced how different my upbringing was compared to some well off friends that I had.

I don't know if there is a name for this phobia or mental disorder for my mindset, but I spent a good portion of my life either judging or feeling like I was being judged. (Probably more the second one, if I'm really honest.) Worrying about what people think about you all the time is draining and can be almost paralyzing.

What I Do Now

When I had some good fortune of my own, I was exposed to successful people and I began to recognize achieving wealth doesn't just happen. Even if you inherit a bunch of money you still need to know how to manage it.

I read a book by Lynne Twist called *The Soul of Money* that was helpful for me and my relationship to understanding money. It taught me how neutral money truly is and how it can be a burden whether you have very little of it or if you have a lot of it and are afraid of losing it. I also read Marianne Williamson's book *The Law of Divine Compensation* and she really opened up my eyes to the idea of being a spiritual person and having an abundant life.

Over time, I basically shifted into a mindset where I was *happy for* people who have wealth. I am no longer jealous or judgmental towards them. I don't compare my economic status to that of others and as a result I feel more peace and appreciation for who I am and for the wonderful things that I have. I understand now my value and what I have to offer the world.

The moral of the story is that we can all improve our finances with focus, taking action, and having faith God has our back. We get to pick the rate at which we receive the abundance. We can take tiny baby steps of receiving and by knowing there is always enough. Slowly but surely the beliefs that cause us to be too materialist versus spiritual dissipate.

If you can afford to buy a new Escalade, I think this is really exciting, but also know if you are getting it to fill some sort of void, then I think the happiness it brings will only be temporary and in the long run isn't going to fill a long term void. In the meantime, realize true joy and bliss come from your heart and your connection to God. Those feelings can't be bought at a car dealership.

I believe it's great if you are attracting and co-creating abundance into your life and can enjoy physical rewards for your efforts, but it is important to understand your relationships with people (and not just stuff) is what delivers fulfillment and a sense of purpose to life.

Baubles and luxury are nice. But don't let the pursuit of material possessions distract you from the fact that you are really an infinite being connected to the Divine.

Father Distortion Number Four—Self-Righteous

We're all perfectly imperfect and I think it is important to realize that even though we are doing personal development work and trying to improve ourselves, we are all equal in the mind of God! One of us isn't more special than the other. We all have a unique purpose. Unfortunately I think people confuse and misinterpret a lot of things in the world because of their self-righteous views.

Nothing bothers me more these days than someone who thinks they are spiritually superior to someone else.

I don't want to lump all religious people together here, but I've definitely been exposed to self-righteous men who have the need to convince people their religious views are right.

Like I mentioned in this section's introduction, the core desire of the Father Wake Rider is to be believed. I think there is good and potentially bad in this core desire. It is wonderful to be a great example to your kids and pass on wisdom, but I feel the problem occurs when a man feels he is always right and not open to other perspectives. Or if he feels he has some moral fiber that makes him better than others because of his convictions and I guess it is their *rigidity* that bothers me.

One thing I've discovered: a person who's religious isn't necessarily better or more moral than someone who is not religious.

My college friend Tom is a good example of this. He's a great dad, and he employs several people in his business. He helps provide for these people's livelihood and he cares for his employees as if they were his own family. Even though his industry is changing he's worked hard at reinventing his company in order to keep as many people employed as possible. He also is more interested in the people that work for him versus just filling a specific job function. These are just a few examples of how he operates with ethics and puts people first.

He's an atheist and he's not religious. Some might then assume he doesn't have very high morals. But on the contrary, he has excellent morals and is a very compassionate person. So the big question is this: does it matter if he goes to church or not on Sunday? Does it matter whether he can quote the Bible or not? He lives by the Golden Rule: "Do unto others as you would have done unto yourself."

Some people believe their religion is right and other religions are wrong. Regardless of if you are Muslim, Christian, Hindu, Buddhist, Mormon, or someone that just believes in science, these are all systems of belief. Each has its own unique positive characteristics. Also, each of these religions have followers who go to extremes on how they interpret the teachings of their holy book. They also have followers who are moderate in their belief and not radical and so it's important to not stereotype each member of a religion.

In my opinion what matters is to be tolerant and respect what everyone's religious *flavor* is, and realize about 70-80% of people probably subscribe to their religious beliefs simply because of their parents or the region of the world they were born in.

I may be coming across as harsh or even judging religious people, but I really respect *all* religions. I truly admire devotional people who spend time in prayer and in service to others. Please don't think I'm anti-religion, I just believe religions are systems of belief which help people try to understand God and commune with Spirit, and it can be done in numerous ways. I don't think there is just one path, or that only one religion is the right religion.

I'm working on a documentary called *Look Beyond Religion* and the purpose of the film is to teach religious tolerance through educating people about prayer. I hope to showcase the most popular prayers in the world. I think it is fascinating to learn about other people's theological beliefs and my goal is to document this passion of mine and hopefully educate some people along the way.

Spirituality is about our connection with God and there are many paths to God because God is everywhere and in everything.

The bottom line is this, we are all equal in the mind of God because we all have a purpose and have unique gifts and talents that contribute to the whole. Think about it: Jesus washed his disciples' feet. There are few other examples that I am aware of that are as powerful, which illustrates how we are all equal. The illusion of thinking one person is better than another because of their spiritual beliefs all comes from ego not connection to God. A sense of superiority also applies to new age spiritual people too. I've witnessed a subtle sense of egoic behavior with these people too where they silently judge people because they think they are more evolved.

Self-righteousness in my opinion seems to create a division among us and that is why it bugs me so much. What all this divisiveness is doing is keeping us in the illusion of being separate from each other and separate from God. In my opinion, spirituality is about unity and being one with God and each other. The first step is not needing to be right. When we must be right all the time, we are creating a *You versus Me* division instead of an *Us* situation of unity.

What I Did Before

I've always felt like God has had a place in my life, but honestly, I never really understood the enormity of the meaning behind this holy connection. I guess I kept God compartmentalized because I've had so much guilt and shame in my past. When I prayed as a parochial student, I just rifled through the words and didn't know what I was saying and was completely incapable of feeling anything. Going to church was always just something I did out of obligation and rushed through the motions as a young man.

I went on to develop a sense that I was better than other people because I somehow had more moral fiber than others because I always tried to be a good guy. No matter how you slice it, this had to do with my good ol' ego.

What I Do Now

Our ego is a big part of who we are and not going anywhere. The trick in my opinion is to slow down enough to become the Observer of our ego. I believe having practices such as breathwork, meditation, sound therapy, praying, earthing, journaling, and yoga, can help us with this slowing down process.

Once I began to accept the ritualistic part of who I am, I allowed myself to invest the time to be a very devotional person, I gave myself permission to put the ritu*al into the word spiritual.* I began to really see how valuable this part of myself was and I began to understand the vastness of my soul and how far it reaches beyond what can be seen in the physical world. I can truly feel the connection now to God when I pray.

My mentor Dianna once told me that I needed to make every day count. I never really figured out how to do that until recently. What I realize is that by having a devotional practice my senses are really sharpening. I've incorporated things such as coherent sound, smell, and light into my practices and this helps expand my awareness in sensing and experiencing the unseen world. Making the time for these rituals is indeed what is helping me make each day count.

As a result of this practice, many of the feelings of spiritual superiority and worrying about who is right or not seems to have become very trivial to me. I now see these distorted beliefs of mine for what they were, which was my ego being afraid. And with this awareness their intensity faded and dissolved into a place of acceptance for everyone.

Spirituality is such an important topic because people feel so strongly about their beliefs, which in turn create biases that are perpetuated from one generation to the next.

That is why the topic of legacy is important to fathers and this is what I will talk about next.

Rider Reminders

- We don't have to live like peasants
- Be open to other's viewpoint
- Spirituality is about feeling connected to something bigger than ourselves

Chapter Fifteen—The *Only* Thing a Father Owes His Children

"Legacy is not leaving something for people. It's leaving something in people." —Peter Strople [19]

Father Ideal Number Three—Legacy-Minded

While we are all unique men, one thing we all have in common is that our physical body has an expiration date. When we can get real with this, and not be afraid of death, we can leverage a new mindset which can help us focus on having a purpose and achieve lifelong goals.

I've struggled with the idea of motivation because it always felt like there was someone looking over my shoulder telling me what I had to do. Like there was some sort of condition I needed to adhere to and there wasn't much choice in the matter. It utterly felt like my free will was taken away.

You may be thinking, "What does this have to do with legacy?" Well, instead of just trudging through life and just getting by, I now ask myself, "What is going to outlast my physical presence? I now wonder what will my kids and other people remember about me when I'm worm food?" I'm starting to feel more focused and energized because I want to create expressive things like books, movies, and music that can outlive me. I feel blessed to be a deep thinker and I feel like I'm supposed to share my ideas. I'm not going to be physically on earth forever, and I'm finally ready to get cracking. This book is a big example of focused attention and drive to produce tangible outcomes.

There is something about having a sense of urgency that can laser-focus your energy and attention to get stuff finished. The bottom line is this: when I'm on my deathbed, I don't want to be disappointed by all the great ideas I had but never brought them into the physical world. But it goes even beyond the physical things we leave behind.

What I Did Before

I used to think legacy mostly had to do with the inheritance you left behind to your family. That a good father works hard to make as much money as possible to not only provide a better life than he had for his kids, but also leave a big stack of cash that helps set up his grandkids too.

There are many experts out there you can get financial advice from so that's not the purpose of this chapter. Trust me, you don't want my advice on money making.

At the pinnacle of my career with a focused legacy belief, I worked for a really rich man named Joe. He's by far the wealthiest person I ever met. He has a great work ethic that truly resulted in creating an empire for himself and his family. I was lucky to see the inner workings of what it takes to create massive financial wealth. I was fortunate enough to go on business trips with him and travel on his private jets (he had three). My favorite was the Challenger because the flights were the smoothest, and unlike a lot of private jets, you could stand all the way up when you moved about the cabin. This was truly a luxurious way to travel and I am so grateful to have had these experiences. There is nothing like pulling your car right up to a plane and throwing your bag right into the stowaway compartment yourself.

During one of our inflight conversations, Joe mentioned to me the only thing a father owes his children "is an education." I took it very literally at the time. I mistakenly thought he meant a father's obligation was to pay for his kid's college tuition. It was a little odd as I thought about Joe and his humble beginnings and realized he didn't go to college. I'm not even sure if any of his three sons finished college either. The correlation I made between college and education was wrong.

It confounded me because he could have easily talked about the millions of dollars he will be leaving behind to his kids and grandchildren. He could have talked about his Foundation and the impact that will have after he is long gone.

What I Do Now

My belief around legacy has shifted dramatically. One day recently it dawned on me what Joe was wisely referring to was that your legacy is more about the wisdom and beliefs you're passing on to your children, and that this *education* was what counted. He was inferring that we teach by our example and the environment we create is what helps our children succeed.

Joe's views, attitudes, and how he led by example, are what is going to live on after he is gone and will last long after the private jets and big houses deteriorate and collapse into scrap. I can only imagine he passed on to his family the importance of learning and embracing the teaching experiences life presents. I imagine he taught them how to handle fear and what really matters in life.

There's a teaching component to legacy most people don't think about. As I've gotten older, I've realized the best teachers are always learning and are just inviting people to come along on the adventure with them. They treat each person as an equal. The teacher is a collaborator and open to expand their own knowledge by listening to everyone, even young people

Legacy can also be the opposite of all of this. A father can pass on his fears and scarcity mindset. This can get bred generation after generation into a family. The words used and the intention behind them are as plain as day but profound regarding the long-term effect they have.

The environment you create as a father is so important. Bruce Lipton talks a lot about this in his epic book *The Biology of Belief.* A father's misperception about lack, unfairness, and the need for justice can be as damaging to generations of children as much as material abundance can be a leg up for wealthy kids. In essence, we are living our legacy every day through the standards and examples we express to our kids.

Another aspect of legacy is the concept of being of service and our willingness to be generous. I spoke about spirituality in the last chapter but will mention here that I feel many religions kind of guilt trip us into being meek, humble, and not greedy. It's important to mention legacy involves being philanthropic and sharing our blessings. Whether it's through charitable giving to churches or creating foundations, having the capacity to serve is a big part of our legacy.

What I Did Before

After my divorce, I started getting away from having really generous behavior because I'd been struggling financially (funny how that works). I also began to feel a little overwhelmed with the idea of a type of moral obligation required of me if I had become successful. It seemed as if this obligation was a requirement to become financially abundant. I also thought that I might become tainted somehow if I became famous or rich.

My good friend Gary said to me one time "Religion preaches not to be materialistic, but they still need wealthy donors to help them build their big churches, support the ministers, and without the rich people there wouldn't be any churches." So, um yeah wow, how true is this? How does that work?

I woke up one morning hearing a voice saying to me "With great power comes responsibility." Throughout the day, this inner voice kept repeating the phrase in my head, as if it was a puzzle or something that I needed to find a solution to. For a bit, it made me think that in order to have power you had to take an oath or something. I got a weird idea that maybe powerful people were bequeathed with some unnatural ability by a secret organization that meets in a castle at a big round table deciding which people get to be wealthy and which people have to stay poor.

Then as my thoughts continued to drift that day I told myself, "No wonder I'm not powerful, who wants to be responsible, anyway?"

I continued to play around with the riddle and I began to scramble the words a little. I flipped around the word responsibility. What came to mind was "ability respond" and then it occurred to me: our ability to respond is a byproduct of our success and not this dreaded *thing* we have to commit to in order to be successful.

What I Do Now

Consequently, as mystical as this experience seemed, a few days later I eventually realized the quote "with great power comes responsibility" was a line from a Spider-Man movie. So much for having a mystical experience where I heard the voice of God.

On a more serious note, what has been showing up for me now is that I really am ready to be more responsible. I can now reflect on how I am the one who made the decisions in the past and I am now willing to accept the consequences for the choices that didn't turn out well and with this awareness I can move forward with even more discernment.

This new *ability to respond* viewpoint is more fun and inspiring to me. It makes me want to have the grit and determination to succeed on *my* terms. It gives me the feeling that God is conspiring *with* me and helping me along the way and not judging me. This has removed some resistance to achieving success. And now I want to really be able to respond should someone approach me with a need.

When you have the resources to serve, it really completes the Law of Circulation which is about the flow that takes place naturally and sustains the energy of receiving and giving. In other words, you literally have the ability to respond to others in need by giving back, and you keep the abundance flowing versus hoarding your money.

I'm starting to be more giving again. Although I don't have a ton of money to just give away willy-nilly, now when situations pop up to give, I do.

This is a wonderful feeling to experience because you can witness the energy of this versus seeing only the material side of the exchanges. When you open up and you're willing to share, this gift creates space for more abundance to flow and it can serve you and others. In addition to being a nice person, being generous shows Source you trust it to fill the space you created by giving away some of your resources.

Recently my GPS redirected me because I missed my exit on the highway. A woman who appeared to be around seven months pregnant was standing on a corner holding a *Will work for food* sign. No one was in sight and I felt like it was divine timing showing up when I did. I gave her a few bucks. It wasn't much but it was all I had on me.

I feel like it was my willingness to give and acknowledge her as a human that illustrates our potential as a soul. Instead of looking down at my phone at the stoplight and ignoring her, there was an exchange of energy. Isn't this why we're here? For me, personally, it's a shift of consciousness from thinking *Man, I only have a little bit and don't have anything to spare,* to knowing *even though I don't have a lot right now, I do have faith in God, and I'll be okay. I'll be supported.* And with this shift in mindset, more prosperity is mysteriously beginning to show up in my life.

When I think about times in my previous abundant life —when I was married and we had two incomes—I remember we consistently gave to our church so consistently, in fact, we were one of the first to do automatic bank withdrawal for our church.

I do wonder if it's one of those *chicken or egg* situations as to what led to what—having the extra money led to the willingness to give, or the willingness to give led to the extra money in our lives?

Father Distortion Number Five—Apathy

What is the opposite of legacy? If one aspect of legacy is about our ability to respond, one opposite would be not doing anything even though we have the means to. I feel like this is what the distortion of apathy is about.

Dictionary.Com defines apathy as:
1. absence or suppression of passion, emotion, or excitement.
2. lack of interest in or concern for things that others find moving or exciting.

You could say some people are too greedy to give, but for the sake of this discussion, I feel we are talking about apathy when one has the financial means to be giving but doesn't because they have no interest in helping people.

What do I think about apathy on a deeper level? To me, it feels like you are stuck, and you are not even alive. You are just going through the motions day by day. You don't grow and learn because your life is lacking passion. I might even go so far as to say true love doesn't exist in an apathetic person's life.

I had an acquaintance of mine die from cancer recently, and he was relatively young (in his forties) and it was his third bout with cancer. When I heard he was really struggling this time around I asked if I could meet him in his office to get to know him on a deeper level and he agreed. When we got together, I asked him how he was doing and how he handled this battle. He told me he was subscribing to the stoic philosophy. I hadn't heard of the stoic philosophy before, so after our meeting I read up on it to learn more. According to *Merriam-Webster's online dictionary,* a stoic is:

> 1: a member of a school of philosophy founded by Zeno of Citium about 300 B.C. holding that the wise man should be free from passion, unmoved by joy or grief, and submissive to natural law.
> 2: one apparently or professedly indifferent to pleasure or pain.

I understand the idea about being even keel and not getting too high or too low, and even being dispassionate about certain things…but man, living with no passion and unmoved by grief or joy? This kind of feels like a waste of life. I don't mean any disrespect for my friend with cancer. He fought it three times and I think I understand why he would subscribe to this way of thinking in the late stages of battling cancer. My point is that I'd never before met anyone that lived by the stoic philosophy and it seems like if you lived this way you would just be going through the motions and not getting the most out of life.

Apathy seems pretty similar to stoicism to me. We probably all have moments of apathy after all, and so let's ask Google "How to overcome apathy"

Here is an article which seems most relevant to the question- https://www.wikihow.com/Stop-Being-Apathetic

Here are the main bullet points of the solutions they recommend-

- Break the cycle. First and foremost, you must decide to break the cycle of apathy.
- Identify the root cause of your apathy. What has taken the wind out of your sails? Have you dealt with a lot of rejection? Was that compounded by your belief that no one listens to you?
- Listen to family and friends. If you hear family and friends trying to "help you" get motivated, they have noticed something might be wrong.
- Examine your isolation. Are you spending the majority of your day by yourself with little to no input from others? Spending the entire day with only your thoughts limits your perception of your life and the world.
- Determine if you are unfairly comparing yourself to others. Apathy is often linked with feelings of unworthiness and can be made worse by constant comparisons to others.
- Examine the things you used to enjoy. Remind yourself what you enjoy doing. Create a list of your joys from the past.

I believe we probably all have times in our life when we choose to be apathetic perhaps as a survival mechanism. My intention is not to judge the reasons, but to identify these behaviors so we can be aware of them if they are causing issues in our life.

The last thing I want to say about apathy is that life is a gift and if we live like a robot eeking out a living, and so attached to our day-to-day routines, we aren't giving a very good example to our kids.Father

Father Distortion Number Six—Skepticism

Being apathetic is a passive distortion of the legacy ideal. So what would be the aggressive distortion?

Skepticism.

If this sounds like a stretch, stay with me: I mentioned before that legacy has a teaching component to it. What happens when we teach our children our doubtful and skeptical views of the world?

What I Did Before

At times, I can seem obsessed regarding if a teacher is authentic or not, which has created a sense of skepticism in me that gets in the way of the message or lesson being taught. Sometimes I spend too much time wondering if the person is legit or not and the learning opportunity gets blocked because I'm distracted. While I think being able to discern and being aware of the dynamics of a situation is important, I also think being overly skeptical gets in the way of learning. Sometimes this doubt even prevents action.

My point? Sometimes you need to take a leap of faith and be open to people's suggestions or what they're trying to share with us.

Being skeptical all the time leads to a *glass-half-empty* mindset. You see this in men when they feel like they've seen it all and think, "If it's too good to be true, then it probably is." There's practicality to this mindset for sure, but it also suffocates any magic that might happen in the natural unfolding of events. More importantly, in the grand scheme of things, kids pick up on how parents act and skepticism gets passed on to the kids inadvertently—and the kids end up robbed of the magic of being a kid.

I think a good example of what I'm trying to explain here is Lucy Van Pelt from the Peanuts cartoons. Lucy is this pessimistic kid who is bossy and opinionated and bullies Charlie Brown. Somewhere along the line poor Lucy had the magic of being a kid robbed from her. Maybe her parents were too busy being overly pragmatic realists and it rubbed off on her.

What I Do Now

Instead of being consumed by skepticism when I receive new information, I exercise a little discernment and I take away what works for me and leave behind what doesn't jive with my current beliefs. I don't get caught up much in the drama of wondering how authentic people are so much anymore. When it comes to influencers and teachers, my view is that if the person's intention is to help others and make the world a better place, then more power to them. It has taken a lot of work, but I'm not in a judging skeptical place as often anymore.

The other way this shows up relates to how we live in a world of skeptics. Everyone wants to debunk something in their pursuit of truth—It's like a badge of honor to be able to point something suspicious out or prove someone wrong. Sometimes this way of thinking is justified, but other times the person pointing out the flaws just ends up looking like a jerk or a fool.

How does this apply to legacy? I think a lot of people don't trust wealthy people and their foundations. People seem to lose sight of the intention behind the philanthropic efforts. The bitter skeptic just sits back and says things like "he's just doing it for the tax write off" or "I've never trusted that guy, he's probably trying to pull off a scam" or "he's doing that just for the PR or political favors."

Their skepticism blinds them from seeing the beauty of the act of giving. They don't see what good the foundation or donation is doing to serve others. In the big picture, the wealthy person didn't have to do anything to help people. There seems to be jealousy towards wealthy people who are building their legacy through giving back. If their heart is in the right place and being generous makes them feel good, and they are just acknowledging how blessed they are, I think this is very admirable. Can we just leave it at that?

I think a prime example of social skepticism is the Gates Foundation. I honestly don't know if the claims and conspiracies are valid or not, but there are a lot of people who question the motives of Bill Gates and his desire to be involved with people's health. Is he wanting to give back or is he trying to do something sinister? I think we are split right down the middle on this one, and we may never find out to be honest with you, but it proves my point about how skeptical we are as a society.

Class envy is a very real thing in our world. It is related to a scarcity mindset. We think it is unfair that one family has more than the next and we buy into the idea that there is only so much to go around. I talk about scarcity in detail in the next chapter which is about infinity.

Rider Reminders

- We live our legacy every single day. It's not an end of life thing. The examples we set and what we teach people is what lasts.
- We are creating memories and people will remember how we made them feel.
- One of the greatest joys in our life is having the ability to respond to help people in need.

Chapter Sixteen—My *New* Superpower

"Life is not about finding our limitations; it's about finding our infinity." —Herbie Hancock

[20]

Father Ideal Number Four—Infinite

Each year for some reason I have a sort of theme that shows up throughout the year. In 2019, I started to really begin thinking a lot about infinity and what it might look like. Instead of being passive and saying "Well, it's all just a mystery." I began using my imagination and examples of this popped into my head. I set the intention of receiving more new ideas and told myself "I'm ready to really see the stuff teachers have been talking about for the last fifty years."

I believe this mindset really was beneficial to my creative work, as it gave me more confidence by understanding there are unlimited possibilities to work with. Usually, when I talk to people about infinity, they just kind of shrug their shoulders and say, "It's infinite…it's beyond our imagination to even know." The curious, childlike nature in me thinks their reply is just kind of a cop-out. My feeling is why not ask the question "What would infinity look like?" This way of thinking can really lead to some fun brainstorming activities when doing creative work.

It occurred to me that infinity is about the mechanics of expansion. I had a realization that free will is at the core of this mechanism. When we are given free will it implies the need to have available choices to choose from. In addition to the initial choice, when you make a decision it opens up a door to another choice and another choice that are all dependent on each choice you make.

It's like a mystical game of *The Prize is Right* and you get to pick from door number one, two, or three. You choose door number three because it's your favorite number and the announcer says "Ginger, show our contestant what's behind door number three." When they open the door, there is a 1974 burnt orange Pinto and now you have a whole new set of choices that didn't exist before. Will you drive it yourself or give it to your niece in college? Will you paint it olive green (another popular color of the '70s) or enter it into a demolition derby? I feel like a byproduct of decision-making and this unfolding of choices, is a never ending expansion that goes on and on every time a choice is made. Therefore, I feel this mechanism ensures infinity is actualized.

There seems to be a symbiotic relationship between free will and the expansion of the unseen world. It's like we are playing the role of co-creator because of our choices. If we didn't have free will and the capacity to decide, everything would be limited and then eventually reality would break.

It feels like God created these replication mechanisms to not only ensure survival but to also have infinite expansion. I've illustrated this idea to people by talking about apples. You can count the seeds in an apple, but not the number of apples in a seed. One seed can create an apple tree, and this tree can have hundreds of apples on it in just one season, let alone thousands of apples in its lifetime. Each one of those apples has a handful of seeds that in turn can grow into another apple tree, and it potentially can go on and on for infinite generations.

What causes this? What is this invisible intelligence which exists innately in everything? In my opinion, it is a form of energy and *recipes* for creation. One might even think about blueprints or templates existing inside of everything. Bruce Lipton talks a lot about DNA and how it holds the blueprint to tell cells how to duplicate. He also goes on to say DNA relies on proteins to be activated by a signal. What is the signal? It is a form of energy and possibly a wake.

I wrote a little about energy in the "Warrior' section and in the "Extras" section of this book in "Understanding Energy."

Everything is energy. I also know through the Observer effect whatever I focus on will perpetuate my circumstances. It can really work for us if we are focused on expansion and creating. Inadvertently it is working against us if our thoughts and observations are based on lack, fear, and everything going wrong. When that wake appears the Rider has a choice on how he is going to ride it. Will he ride it with fear or with confidence?

This phenomenon is designed to perpetuate life and it is neutral. The wake doesn't care how much money the Rider has in his bank account or if he has perfect abs and a hot wife. It is going to keep moving on and on no matter how the Rider is showing up in life.

Infinity consciousness isn't necessarily a god choosing who gets to be the favored ones like some religions want you to believe. When the Bible talks about God and the chosen ones, in my opinion, it should talk about God favors the *choosers*! Whether we are aware of it or not, we are all choosers. I'm not saying there isn't a God, but I am saying, free will is a default setting. Free will has more to do with the quantum mechanics necessary to ensure life replicates and survives infinitely, and not because we are superior, deserve anything, or privileged in some way.

What is exciting to me is that *everyone* can tap into this phenomenon. This way of thinking really gives a scientific basis on how abundance is actualized. Some people call this "life force energy," but I prefer the gentler term of "life *source* energy." I can tap into this infinite source of ideas, inspirations, solutions, serendipities, and flow. This doesn't affect you one iota. The pie is infinite. There is enough for everyone.

The ideas of lack and scarcity only exist in this realm when it is focused on and given attention. Our ego-driven world of fear focuses on lack! Sin is missing your mark. You were focusing on the wrong thing when you *sinned*. So, move away from focusing on lack. When you focus on it you are missing your mark. None of this has anything to do with morals or greed. This is quantum mechanics.

Infinity consciousness can impact the way business is done. When we move away from scarcity thinking and into a more prosperous philosophy, the fear of being *attacked* by our competition goes away. When we make this shift in our thinking it then opens us up to the idea of collaboration versus competition. Our imagination now has a whole new sandbox to play in. Think about this a moment, what if your biggest *competitor* could become an ally and potentially help you get better at what you do? How amazing is this idea?

There is a business psychology emerging called Blue Ocean Theory. I personally love this term because it reminds me of surfing and how we show up. A blue ocean is a new market that never existed before. Many things in technology illustrate this concept. Twenty four years ago, there were no cell phone apps. The concept didn't even exist until smartphones were invented. Now there are thousands of apps if not hundreds of thousands of apps. Also, think about pop sockets, selfie sticks, photo filters, and cell phone stabilizers made popular because of social media. How many millions of dollars in sales are being generated now by these things and they didn't even exist five or six years ago?

The Blue Ocean Theory is a real thing, and it has a lot to do with acknowledging there is an infinite source of new ideas to be tapped into, and so why do we even worry about competition?

I know for a fact the highest caliber of creative work I've done is always the result of working with others. I think I can tap into Source and have some pretty cool stuff come through on my own, but when I open myself up to get others' opinions and ideas on improving my "baby" even more magic happens. In essence, I'm open to observing their unseen world and frankly maybe assisting them in seeing it too.

If you believe all things are already created in the unseen world, the real magic happens when you open yourself up to see it and not try to control what shows up.

Recently, I was freaking out about the unknown. One thing I thought was "what if I became uber-successful and what if I would turn into someone I didn't recognize?" I thought about the other end of the spectrum too by the way. This way of thinking was really holding me back. Thankfully, I realized this fear of the unknown was slowing me down and causing me not to finish this book. But then I started to think about infinity and how infinity IS the unknown because it is so huge. The unknown should not be feared is what I told myself, and I then realized we just can't know what something is until we are in an expanded state. Unknown = Potential.

Infinity means I get to learn stuff straight from the unknown which technically is a source that no one else has seen either. I can move past all the Law of Attraction stuff like creating a vision board. Instead, I know infinity is beyond what I paste on a poster in my bedroom. When we attempt to dictate to the quantum the exact endpoints and exact *how's*, we are limiting infinity down to just those. It is okay to have desires and conspire with the unseen world, but equally, it is important to realize the unknown is part of all things. Now I see the unknown represents infinite choices and options and the unknown is *beautiful!* Embracing the unknown is like a superpower I now have. All of this gives me peace and helps me not be fearful. It's like when you are a kid and you finally stop worrying about the dark. I hope all of you can feel this now too.

Father Distortion Number Seven—Scarcity Mentality

The Father Wake Rider is all about love and abundance. But infinity includes everything and this includes scarcity consciousness.

There are two types of people in this world: *Scarcity thinkers* who are about the finite and believe reality is a zero-sum game and there is only *so much* of something, and *abundance thinkers* who understand the idea that there is enough for everyone and they tap into infinite ideas all the time.

Scarcity thinkers believe there is only so much money in the world, only so much oil, and only so many acres of land. These people are not looking beyond what's in front of them. They aren't asking the next question. They aren't asking "What's something new that can be created because of this situation?" A scarcity thinker worries about there not being enough land, water, or oil and wastes a lot of their energy worrying about how we are going to theoretically run out of resources.

Conversely, abundance thinkers ask "What's next?" They ask questions like "What are other ways we can access energy?" or "What is a new solution to be had?" They wonder to themselves, "Maybe we can have cars run on solar power or wind power or even water and not just gasoline." There truly is no scarcity for these people because they know that our thoughts are endless.

Scarcity and lack happen when we're not focusing our thoughts on new ideas and new potentials. We really can get stuck. It sucks when this happens, and it's a very real force, like a gravity that holds us down and prevents us from moving forward, keeping us stuck in the fear of the unknown. There is logic and numbers which come into play when you think finitely.

Logic and numbers often appear to support scarcity thinking. Let's think of a finite thought such as the idea that there is only so much food in the world. This thought is very believable. Sadly, many people suffer and even die from starvation every day. Someone could logically prove there's only so much fertile land to farm on, and therefore if the population is too large this finite amount of land just can't support the human need for food.

One may even say there are environmental issues that limit the places we can grow food. If you buy into the idea that there is only so much land, and you accept this as a fact, then guess what? Since your thoughts are finite, your limiting beliefs influence the reality you are observing, and people are going to starve when we focus on scarcity.

What if you looked beyond the idea of a limited amount of land being the problem causing starvation. What if you looked at ideas like better food distribution systems and improving how food gets to people? What if you also thought not just about horizontal space like land and started to look at the infinite amount of vertical space available. And then you realize that environmental conditions are not a problem because every community could grow their food indoors with hydroponic techniques.

There's a creative solution for everything if we change our perspective and ask different questions.

The real magic happens when we maintain this mindset day after day. Having a support system of friends and family is what can help us make this shift and sustain this new thinking. If you apply yourself, there is an infinite flow you can tap into. You have the innate ability to be creative and receive solutions from this infinite intelligence full of ideas if you choose. You can become re-energized when you start opening yourself up to possibilities and being aware of what you are focusing on.

My friend Phylis has a program she created called *"Prosperosophy"* that has a daily affirmation about prosperity. The program includes the idea of our *set point,* a consciousness "thermostat" set to where our comfort zone is. As we grow, we expand and have a new normal as our set point moves to a new, expanded comfort zone and way of being.

All potential is unseen, but as our set point rises, we more consistently *see* the abundance and infinite showing up in our lives. We see proof of how abundant we already are and begin to witness and understand how prosperity shows up. Mysterious things happen, like when a prospect you met two years ago at a bar reaches out to you and says they want to work together now. Abundance can just show up out of nowhere sometimes. This could be called a miracle because it defies logic. I'd like to believe It's providence, or at the very least, serendipity.

Father Distortion Number Eight—Idol Worship

If one of the opposites of an infinity mindset is a scarcity mentality, logic would dictate the other extreme would be greed. I contend it is more about idol worship though. This may seem like a stretch, but idol worship is an inadvertent practice that keeps us playing small and not owning our own potential greatness and therefore an opposite of infinite consciousness.

When I was a kid, I used to collect miniature versions of NFL football helmets. I was a little infatuated by them, now that I think about all the helmets I used to own. My little helmet collection meant a lot to me. You might even say I was truly greedy in wanting more and more of those little helmets.

I was still a really innocent kid and so I wonder, could I really have been capable of greed back then? Isn't greed reserved for rich dudes who are powerful or bad guys like Dr. Evil? I do know I was obsessed with those little helmets though.

The helmets had the team logo on them. They were these gorgeous designs, but it was also what was beyond the design that contained the power. It was the *greatness* this team symbol stood for which was the god-like talents and characteristics of the men who were on the real team. The mini helmet represented the NFL players who wore the uniform in the physical world on the playing field. The modern-day battlefield. These were the best of the best football players in the world. I was worshiping what the little helmet stood for. This is what I feel the real energy and distortion is regarding greed. We want more and more and more and more of a feeling of being able to touch greatness. Being able to touch someone else's greatness is like a surrogate that appeases us because we do not understand our own greatness. Having access and connecting to perfection is what we crave, and we want to feel it inside ourselves, but we really do not know how to attain it for ourselves, and so we latch onto something which symbolizes greatness. The helmet is a ghost. It is a symbol of greatness, but it isn't greatness itself, but we can touch it, and it feels like we can own it, but in reality, we just own the symbol of greatness, and deny that we ourselves are great (the map is not the territory).

We get mesmerized by this idol and we can't see the illusion. All we know is it makes us feel good somehow because we feel we are touching greatness, and we just want more and more of this feeling no matter what.

The interesting thing is some of my initial and very raw creative abilities came during this timeframe of my life. You see, those helmets are what gave me the drive to learn how to draw. It was like I was in such a trance studying their awesomeness, I would hyper-focus on the image and then somehow transmute the vision into a drawing. I spent hours on end perfecting my ability to draw the exact curve of the Rams' emblem. I memorized the subtle difference between the C on the Chicago Bears helmet and the C on the Cincinnati Reds baseball hat. I *loved* drawing the Chargers' lightning bolt.

It would be very easy to jump on the road to the *higher* ground and talk about how greed is bad or immoral. I prefer to observe it and see how it fits into the whole and even try to see the lesson or blessing. If there was some sort of sin here that I can mention, it would be that worshiping idols is related to our need to cling onto perfection. If we can let go of that need I think our life can be a little less disappointing.

I admit it's a bit of a leap for me to say a distortion of an infinite mindset is worshiping idols, but let's go a little deeper into this.

Here is a quote by famed psychologist Erich Fromm that helps drive home my point on why worshiping false idols isn't good:

"The strength of man's position in the world depends on his degree of adequacy of his perception of the world and reality. The less adequate, the more insecure he is and, hence, he is in need of idols to lean on and find security. The more adequate it is, the more he can stand on his own feet and has his center within himself."

What I Did Before

In the past, I've had a really bad habit of putting people up on a pedestal. Subconsciously, I was saying I am inferior in some way to them and we were not equals. I struggled with this a lot when I was young when I had to go to a public school in ninth grade and a lot of my friends went onto private high schools. When this happened there was a shift in me and I began to think they were better than me somehow.

As an adult I pursued mentors and friends who had a special talent or look about them. When I'd be around them I'd try to stay calm but often I'd be really giddy on the inside. They have what the French call *je ne sais quoi*. When I think about this now I guess I was hoping I'd be perceived as being cooler just through my association with these epic people.

Something interesting I found a few years ago is that the majority of people that I consider my best friends are all Libras. When I realized that anomaly I decided to look at the people I put up on a pedestal and discovered each one were Geminis (including the out of my league lover). This all might seem very random and astrological hocus pocus, but what is really intriguing is that both of my parents are Geminis.

What I Do Now

The problem with putting someone on a pedestal is that we are potentially denying our own greatness and our connection to God.

I realize that we can honor talents in others and even *love* this about someone. But I now know that harm is done when we go into the lost space of infatuation and begin chasing the ghost.

Watching a baseball player hit a home run every other day he plays is a thing of beauty don't get me wrong. The fact is this person put hours and hours and hours of practice into sharpening those skills. I honor the practice, and this is a great example of tenacity for all of us. A positive takeaway for me has been to realize how important practice is and there is potential inside of me too to be great at something, too, if I put in the work to learn new skill and hone my craft.

What I do now is work with more focused effort and try to minimize distractions. I am also opening myself up to thinking that I have the ability to make a difference in the world with my work. It might not be colossal, but I'm open to the idea of playing on a bigger stage than I ever have in the past. Clinging on to the idea of feeling inferior has dissolved. My need to put people on pedestals still happens occasionally, but I realize now that these people are my equals. I now desire to be around really strong people and collaborate with them as a peer. This is brand new territory for me. It is exciting and frightening at the same time but feels like where I belong.

Rider Reminders

- Tapping into infinite thinking solves a lot of problems.
- Abundance thinking helps us manage fear and emotions.
- Free will is a mechanical component of infinity that ensures replication and eternal creation.
- One person's abundance doesn't affect my abundance.

Father Section Takeaways

The Fourth B Word—Beyond

The Father Wake Rider is about learning to move beyond fear, judgment, anger, and shame.

The Father Wake Rider looks beyond his physical self and understands his infinite nature and the future impact he'll have on his children and his children's children. He has the ability to look beyond present circumstances and take a leap of faith knowing without any evidence that he'll be supported and that he'll thrive.

He shows us we can look beyond our needs and focus on the needs of others. By knowing he's sharing his talents with his family and community he knows his strength has a purpose.

He knows there's a source he can tap into beyond what his eyes can see in this physical world and he knows that beyond our fears, pain, and uneasiness, infinite love and adventure can show up in our life if we learn to let go.

If you're a father yourself and you're having a hard time with issues like forgiveness and wrapping your head around how you're an example to your children, use the Father B-Word *Beyond* to help you get on course. Let it be your beacon and remind you there is so much beyond who you are in this very moment. Unlimited potential beyond you can be tapped into to bring you to a place of ease and grace.

Rite of Passage

Remember at the beginning of this section I mentioned the Father's desire is to be believed because it's proof that he lived? This is a source of pain for many men if it turns into not knowing if he'll be remembered after he's gone. Even with all the growth we experience in our lives, this is still a deep, unspoken pain men have buried deep in their psyche.

While I was working on the final manuscript of *The Whole Dude* I really got into the idea that we have multiple rites of passage in our lives as men. I stumbled across a report written by Dr. Manu Ampim who wrote about five rites of passage tribes in Africa believe in. The final two best illustrate what I think the Father's Rite of Passage is all about.

Dr. Ampim writes about the Rite of Eldership and the Rite of Ancestorship. In African cultures, the Rite of Eldership is attained when someone has lived a life of honor and purpose and is given the highest status in their culture.

The next distinction has to do with when a person passes away. If a person gets old and dies and isn't an elder, he basically is just a dead relative and eventually forgotten. Consequently, infants and elders are considered the closest links to the spirit world. If someone achieves the distinction of being an elder, upon their death they receive the Rite of Ancestorship which means they will *always* be remembered. African philosophy, from one culture to another, agrees that the spirit of the deceased is still with the living community. Thus, ancestors are respected elders who have passed away yet continue to serve as an extension of the family and community.

This best describes what I think our ultimate existence as men is—to have lived a life of honor and purpose to the degree that not only are you remembered, but you are continued to be referred to as a source of wisdom even after your physical body is gone.

You ultimately become part of the infinite source of life.

Exercise

Is your father alive? If so, have a conversation with him. Tell him you're working on an assignment. Ask him to tell you about what he is most proud of accomplishing and what he regrets the most in his life. Ask him if there is anything he wants to accomplish still. Ask him if he has any advice for you that he's never gotten a chance to give you. If your father is not alive, spend time in meditation and have this conversation with him in the spiritual realm.

Summary

Now that you finished reading *The Whole Dude*, I'd like to add a little more insight to consider related to each Wake Rider.

Specifically, I'd like to spell out how the concepts of choice and acceptance changes with each Wake Rider.

One big wound of the Son I mentioned in the book relates to worrying about being accepted by people. When we can finally move past this immature need, our life can truly change. Regarding choice, in the early stages of his development the Son inherits a lot of beliefs and he doesn't even realize that he himself is allowed to make choices.

In his early stages, the Warrior discovers parents, teachers, and leaders aren't perfect. He realizes that in order to become a victor he needs to be the one making the choices for himself. He begins to carve out expectations of what he wants his life to look like. Instead of worrying about being accepted (like the Son), he learns that he can decide what is acceptable to him. He sets standards for himself and the material things he wants in his life. He creates boundaries and makes sure he is treated well. He gets really good at making choices and develops discernment.

The Lover realizes he can learn a lot from others if he chooses to listen. He becomes aware that other people have expectations, boundaries and standards too. The Lover knows everyone is valuable and he shifts away from being 100% worried about what is *acceptable* to only him. Acceptance becomes more of a barometer to measure his joy. The word "acceptable" can now be cut in half and turned around to now read "able to accept." The Lover develops his capacity of allowing things to unfold naturally and doesn't have to manipulate things to get what he wants.

Choice and acceptance plays a big part of the Father's ability to be mindful. The Father understands infinity and knows there are unlimited options to choose from and that everyone has a unique perspective from which they make choices. He knows that free will is at the foundation of all creation. He knows that without the ability to choose, the existence of life would collapse and with this wisdom he isn't triggered by other people's choices. He can accept everything.

This ability of the Father isn't a sign of weakness. One may feel like this is about surrender, but it is beyond that. This is about expanding our capacity to move about the world not being bothered by irritants and threats. Also when we accept everyone, we are growing because we realize others' perspectives may have unique insights that can broaden our own wisdom. There are infinite perspectives we can tap into.

We are constantly digging and peeling back the layers and learning about ourselves. For me personally, it has been a nostalgic and expansive journey writing this book and frankly I don't even know if I'm the same person that I was when I began this project.

I wanted to be authentic and leave it up to the reader how much they wanted to dig into the meanings of my stories and not try to fix anyone. Having said that, if you are interested in going deeper, I do have course material and a podcast that you can learn about at thewholedude.com.

Thank you again for investing your time, energy, and money to read my book!

EXTRAS

Verification

In an effort to validate that I was on the right path, I revisited models that I'd studied regarding human development. One thing that popped up was the Hawkins Map of Consciousness, which shows the expansion one goes through on their journey to enlightenment. Several of the ideals I've presented are on that map, so having this verification meant a lot to me.

Another tool I reviewed and compared these characteristics to is the Emotional Guidance Scale, which is a diagram that shows how our emotions spiral either upward or downward and so in a way the "ideal" emotions of The Whole Dude are like emotions that are spiraling up and are positive and then the "distortions" are the emotions that are spiraling down.

A new resource that I'm learning about is the *Nine Levels of Ego Development* by Susanne Cook-Greuter. I'm excited to learn more about this because there is a correlation between this report and my Wake Riders' development. She talks about the phases of the ego and these include, pre-conventional, conventional, post conventional and transcendent. The model is a progression of development we go through on a journey of self-actualization. This material is profound and very scientific compared to my casual storytelling. However, I was pretty blown away to receive the verification that my intuition is on track. From what I can tell so far, the things I discuss in *The Whole Dude* align with the beginning of post-conventional stage and comes close to the transcendent stage. The report was based on years of research studying thousands of people around the world. It's pretty dry and reads like a science book, but if you're committed to evolving as a human, I highly recommend you find a copy. (For a more digestible version of this information, check out Leo Gura's work at **Actualized.org**.)

Lastly, I discovered two studies conducted by the National Institute of Health (NIH). Their research showed the correlation between our organ health and our emotions. The

first report was called "Understanding Mind-Body Interaction from the Perspective of Asian Medicine" and the second report was called "Body Maps of Emotions." I found it fascinating that there is research which pinpoints how certain emotions can affect specific parts of our body. Here are the links- https://www.ncbi.nlm.nih.gov/pmc/articles/PMC5585554/
and
https://www.ncbi.nlm.nih.gov/pmc/articles/PMC38961five0/

Understanding Energy

Lately I've sarcastically been saying "Matter doesn't matter."

If you break something down that appears solid to its most basic building blocks of matter, you'll find that inside the molecules there isn't anything except energy and no matter. Albert Einstein was famously quoted as saying "everything is energy and that's all there is to it."

What he was saying is that energy is at the very core of everything.

We get confused by what energy is because we can't really see it. All we can do is experience it through our senses. Also we look at ourselves like the Energizer Bunny and all we consider is if we have enough juice left or if we feel like a dead battery. That's the extent of which most people think about energy.

But I'm a nerd and think about this topic *a lot*. I think so much about it that I'm even starting to make up some of my own theories on how this all works and am getting rather opinionated and disagree with a lot of conventional thinking around energy.

In the intro of this book, I mentioned that everything is in motion. I think that's a good place to start because we can all get our heads around that. We all know that the earth is hurtling through space and therefore we must be in motion. Also, at a molecular level everything is moving. In physics they say everything is either a particle or a wave. This thought is well accepted and has been around for a long time. But here is where my thoughts differ. The theory goes on to say that when a wave is observed it collapses into a particle. This is called the Observer Effect and there have been volumes of quantum physics books written about this.

But here's the deal. Even though I'm not a scientist, I have my own theory. My theory is that the wave never collapses. My belief is that these waves are infinite and act as channels that contain data. I even believe that within the waves are the ideas of God and all of the recipes that keep everything alive. But that is a little bit beyond the scope of this book. At the very least, I believe the only thing scientists could possibly observe is a single data point as the wave passes by.

I also think the wave itself is unperceivable and the observer only sees something like a ghost. More than likely what is going on is that the observer is assigning a meaning to that data point. As I mentioned in the Son section we are correlators. We take data points and connect them to create a meaning. All information is a construct that someone created to give meaning to our reality. I believe we don't even see the wave at all. I feel what we think is a wave is really the wake the wave tossed off when it passed by. What we are reacting to and creating meaning around is the artifact or aftermath of what was only there for the briefest, almost timeless moment.

People mistake the idea of a wave all the time and think we surf waves but we don't. We surf the wake. The wave spins in a twirling three dimensional shape and as that shape cuts through space it stirs up the field and tosses up the wake. Think about the propeller of a boat and how it spins. It spins and churns up the water to create a wake.

I think this is at the foundation of everything.

We are surrounded by these invisible wakes. A lot of people talk about frequency and vibration but sadly I skeptically think they are just parroting something they heard from a guru and they don't really go deep enough on this topic. They leave stuff out. Hardly anyone talks about the other components of a wave such as amplitude, peaks and troughs, and the wave pattern itself. They think of a vibration like it is a radio station or something. They say we vibe together and we are on the same frequency. I kind of gag when I hear that now.

What is really happening is that people are in phase and their movement is in sync. They have a similar awareness that they are each tuning in to and their energy together is congruent. When you're with someone you're "vibing" with, essentially the wake you're each creating together is coherent. It is nice and smooth and feels good. You can't see it but you can sense it. You like their ideas, the way they smell, their appearance, the sound of their voice. These are all the wakes their energy is putting off that you subconsciously pick up on and all you know is that it feels safe and agreeable with you.

If you have *chemistry* with someone, things can really get interesting. If there was dissonance between you and the other person, the wakes you'd be creating are distorted and not smooth and this is incoherent energy. This is when you aren't "vibing" with someone.

Everyone has a unique perspective. How we experience all this invisible stuff is through our senses. We feel a breeze, smell a flower, taste a drink, hear a song, see a color. Every element has a unique energetic signature that is the input we sense, but we interpret the signal. That's why a certain song or a particular scent stirs up memories in us.

We're finely engineered machines that operate off this sensory system. Every cell in our body is listening for signals and discerning if it's a beneficial signal or harmful.

On a macro level, we make meaning out of these signals and our reality is glued together based on the meaning we assign to them. Unfortunately, the signal can be distorted. The meanings we assign make us who we are. We store the meanings in our cellular biology where they accumulate into emotions—there are even correlations between harmful emotions and our organs. Our belief systems and biases affect how we make decisions, navigate what we deem is right or wrong, and determine what feels good or harmful. All at the speed of light.

Getting a grasp of these concepts can be very useful as we surf our life. It is like a new super power when we realize that we can pick up on and truly understand the energy people put off. We also begin to realize that we have the final say and control how we can show up in any given situation.

For years and years, I've been around what people refer to as an *awakening* to the degree that I've even used the word awake in company names and online communities I've built. But what I realize now is that this is about awareness that we have or we don't. It has nothing to do with 5D or an ascension process or any of the stuff new age gurus talk about. I'm kind of sick of when people use the word awake now—I jokingly say to people, "I don't want to be awake, I want to ride a wake."

That's why I call the characters in my book Wake Riders. We choose the energy we want to exhibit as we ride the wakes that come our way in life.

We can approach the wake with wonder and purity like the Son.

We can attack the situation with strength and discernment like a Warrior.

We can embrace and enjoy the sweetness of a wake like a Lover.

We can see beyond our circumstance like the Father.

We have the inalienable right—and the power—to choose how we act and react every moment. When we have this awareness and the ability to integrate all of this in our life, we are a Whole Dude and our life can be truly exquisite.

Acknowledgements

Well to start out, I'm very grateful for my family because slowing down and spending time with them is what has taught me our precious time together is what witnessing and savoring the sweetness of life is all about.

There have been many teachers in my life that have influenced me who have shown up in the form of books, retreats and in person one on one experiences. There are frankly too many to list here. I do have to however give a shout out to the close friends who spent countless hours of their time listening to me, affirming my thoughts, and offering feedback. This list of dear friends include: Eileen Wolfe, Shellie Rosen, Dan Sides, Laura Lynne Dyer, Zisa Henderson, Dorian Cole, Jessie Starr, and Christine McCabe. I owe a huge debt of gratitude to my dear friend Kimberly Schipke who I've had countless conversations with about energy and the unseen world.

I received a lot of assistance with proofing and editing. Early helpers included Laurel Fuller Clark, Brooke Jolley, and Robin Reese. Also, I am grateful for Christine Hepler for helping me with the final proof reading which added that last layer of polish the book needed. And finally I couldn't have finished this book without the help of my new friend and editor Patrick Dorsey. You truly are the best dude!

I've been blessed to be a content producer most of my career and I know my limitations. I am a huge fan of collaboration because it leads to extraordinary outcomes that I simply could not achieve on my own. I would like to thank my illustrator Casey Dilzer for the great job she did drawing each of the Wake Riders. I really felt it'd be good to give everyone a fun visual on the progression of these characters. Also, my lifelong friend (who I mention in the book a couple times) Michael Behrens made himself available for art direction &

feedback and shared his immense talents to take the cover to another level.

The audiobook is another example of collaborating. I was thrilled when the following friends gracefully offered music to sample throughout *The Whole Dude Audiobook* and these included: Bradford Smith, Brandon Salter, Mark Malle, Frequency Matters, and Kevin Jamison. (I really hope we can do future music projects together guys.)

Lastly, thank YOU for the time and money you invested in all of this. I hope you like my stories as much as I enjoyed sharing them.

Book Suggestions

What follows is a list of books that have influenced me over the years:

- The Power of Now
- The Four Agreements
- Zen and the Art of Motorcycle Maintenance
- The No Limit Person
- The New Earth
- Think and Grow Rich
- Soul of Money
- The Law of Divine Compensation
- Stealing Fire
- Awaken the Giant Within
- Seven Habits of Highly Effective People
- The Five Love Languages
- Four Desires by Rod Stryker
- Teachings on Love
- Creative Visualization
- Tender Warrior
- Radical Acceptance
- The Alchemist
- The Power of Intention
- Ask and It Is Given
- The Power of Focus
- A Course in Miracles
- Harmonic Wealth
- Seat of the Soul
- Forgiveness, It isn't what you think it is
- Black Elk Speaks
- The Healer Within
- Celestine Prophecies
- The Field
- Yoga Sutra

References

I felt it would be good to give readers details regarding the quotes I used at the beginning of chapters and sections. It was a very difficult task to find the origins of the quotes and so I included what I felt were interesting bits of information that I found on the web. A lot of this came from either wikipedia.com or from the public figures' website.

1- Many people know the popular Rolling Stones song "Sympathy for the Devil' and might even hum along in their head when they read the Introduction. Many people attribute the success of the band to the dynamic duo of Mick Jagger and Keith Richards but for the most part this song was mostly the creative genius of Jagger. I found this really fascinating article that goes deep into the song on Medium.com in their Legends of Music series. Here is the article: https://medium.com/@thelegendsofmusic/the-story-behind-sympathy-for-the-devil-ad1f7b70410a

2- Dr. Gary Chapman is a well-known marriage counselor and director of marriage seminars. *The 5 Love Languages®* is one of Chapman's most popular titles, topping various bestseller charts for years, selling over twenty million copies and has been on the New York Times bestsellers list since 2007.

3- Rachel Louise Carson (May 27, 1907 – April 14, 1964) was an American marine biologist, author, and conservationist whose influential book *Silent Spring* (1962) and other writings are credited with advancing the global environmental movement. Carson began her career as an aquatic biologist in the U.S. Bureau of Fisheries, and became a full-time nature writer in the 1950s. Her widely praised 1951 bestseller *The Sea Around Us* won her a U.S. National Book Award.

4- As quoted in *After Einstein : Proceedings of the Einstein Centennial Celebration* (1981) by Peter Barker and Cecil G. Shugart, p. 179. The most beautiful thing we can experience is the mysterious. It is the source of all true art and science. He to whom this emotion is a stranger, who can no longer pause to wonder and stand rapt in awe, is as good as dead: his eyes are closed." Also quoted in *Introduction to Philosophy* (1935) by George Thomas White Patrick and Frank Miller Chapman, p. 44. "The most beautiful emotion we can experience is the mysterious. It is the fundamental emotion that stands at the cradle of all true art and science. He to whom this emotion is a stranger, who can no longer wonder and stand rapt in awe, is as good as dead, a snuffed-out candle. To sense that behind anything."

5- John Winston Lennon; 9 October 1940 – 8 December 1980) was an English singer, songwriter, musician and peace activist who achieved worldwide fame as the founder, co-songwriter, co-lead vocalist and rhythm guitarist of the Beatles. Lennon was characterized by the rebellious nature and acerbic wit in his music, writing and drawings, on film, and in interviews. His songwriting partnership with Paul McCartney remains the most successful in history. Born in Liverpool, Lennon became involved in the skiffle craze as a teenager. In 1956, he formed the Quarrymen, which evolved into the Beatles in 1960.

6- Walt Whitman's family papers span forty years from 1852 (three years before the first publication of *Leaves of Grass*) to the end of Whitman's life in 1892. A highlight in the series is the 1863 diary written by Whitman's brother George (1829-1901), who served in a New York regiment of the Union Army in the Civil War. Whitman was especially close to George and to their younger brother Jeff (1833-1890), who lived and worked in St. Louis.

7- Booker T. Washington published a series of autobiographical articles in the New York periodical *The Outlook*. On November 10, 1900, the quote that I mentioned was in Volume 66, Number 11 in a piece called *Up from Slavery: An Autobiography by Booker T. Washington*.

8- As quoted in *Diversity : Leaders Not Labels* (2006) by Stedman Graham, p. 224. Maya Angelou was an American poet, memoirist, and civil rights activist. She published seven autobiographies, three books of essays, several books of poetry, and is credited with a list of plays, movies, and television shows spanning over 50 years. She received dozens of awards and more than 50 honorary degrees.

9- Bob Marley (1945-1981) was an internationally acclaimed Jamaican reggae musician, Rastafarian, and Pan-Africanist. Due to his success, first with The Wailers and then during his solo career, the Marley name has become nearly inseparable with reggae and the Rastafari religion. Marley, who remains a beloved symbol of peace and music, died of cancer in 1981 at the young age of 36.

10-Born to an aristocratic Russian family in 1828, Leo Tolstoy's notable works include the novels *War and Peace* (1869) and *Anna Karenina* (1878), often cited as pinnacles of realist fiction. He first achieved literary acclaim in his twenties with his semi-autobiographical trilogy, *Childhood, Boyhood, and Youth* (1852–1856), and *Sevastopol* Sketches (1855), based upon his experiences in the Crimean War. His fiction includes dozens of short stories and several novellas such as *The Death of Ivan Ilyich* (1886), *Family Happiness* (1859), *After the Ball* (1911) and *Hadji Murad* (1912). He also wrote plays and numerous philosophical essays.

11- Many people feel a defining moment of John Kennedy's presidency was his 1961 Inaugural Speech where his most famous quote "Ask not what your country can do for you – ask what you can do for your country" was at the climax of his speech. He also said the quote I mentioned about diplomacy and I feel that quote is just as poignant.

12- Born in central Vietnam in 1926, Thich Nhat Hanh entered Tu Hieu Temple, in Hue city, as a novice monk at the age of sixteen. As a young bhikshu (monk) in the early 1950s he was actively engaged in the movement to renew Vietnamese Buddhism. He was one of the first bhikshus to study a secular subject at university in Saigon, and one of the first six monks to ride a bicycle. Hanh passed away just recently (Jan 2022).

13- This quote comes from the *Happy Birthday Book*. The bulk of Theodor Seuss Geisel's books were published under the name of Dr. Seuss. The exceptions include Great Day for Up!, My Book about ME, Gerald McBoing Boing, *The Cat in the Hat Beginner Book Dictionary* (credited to the Cat himself), 13 books credited to Theo. LeSeig, *Because a Little Bug Went Ka-Choo!* and *I Am Not Going to Get Up Today!*, though all were in fact illustrated and written by Geisel.

14- Shannon Kaiser is the best-selling author of five books on the psychology of happiness and fulfillment including T*he Self-Love Experiment* and *Adventures for Your Soul, Joy Seeker*, and *Unshakable Inner Peace Oracle card deck*, and the forthcoming book *Return to You*. She has a B.A. in journalism and communications from the University of Oregon. As an international life coach, speaker, and retreat leader, she helps people awaken and align with their true selves so they can live their highest potential.

15- In 1952 Marie Beynon Ray published *The Best Years of Your Life* and the quote is on page 82, in which she discussed enjoying a full life during retirement years. The full quote is: "But we are not living in eternity. We have only the present moment, sparkling like a star in our hands — and melting like a snowflake."

16- Helen Adams Keller was born a healthy child in Tuscumbia, Alabama, on June 27, 1880. Her parents were Kate Adams Keller and Colonel Arthur Keller. On her father's side she was descended from Colonel Alexander Spottswood, a colonial governor of Virginia, and on her mother's side, she was related to a number of prominent New England families. Helen's father, Arthur Keller, was a captain in the Confederate army. The family lost most of its wealth during the Civil War and lived modestly. After the war, Captain Keller edited a local newspaper, the North Alabamian, and in 1885, under the Cleveland administration, he was appointed Marshal of North Alabama.

At the age of 19 months, Helen became deaf and blind as a result of an unknown illness, perhaps rubella or scarlet fever. As Helen grew from infancy into childhood, she became wild and unruly.

17- Publilius Syrus (fl. 85–43 BC[1]), was a Latin writer, best known for his sententiae. He was a Syrian from Antioch who was brought as a slave to Roman Italy. Syrus was brought to Rome on the same ship that brought Manilius the astronomer and Staberius Eros the grammarian. By his wit and talent, Syrus won the favor of his master, who granted him manumission and educated him. He became a member of the Publilia gens. Publilius' name, due to the palatalization of 'l' between two 'i's in the Early Middle Ages, is often presented by manuscripts (and some printed editions) in corrupt form as 'Publius', Publius being a very common Roman praenomen.

18- Carl Edward Sagan (November 9, 1934 – December 20, 1996) was an American astronomer, planetary scientist, cosmologist, astrophysicist, astrobiologist, author, and science communicator. His best known scientific contribution is research on extraterrestrial life, including experimental demonstration of the production of amino acids from basic chemicals by radiation. Sagan assembled the first physical messages sent into space, the Pioneer plaque and the Voyager Golden Record, universal messages that could potentially be understood by any extraterrestrial intelligence that might find them.

The quote I mention is from the book *The Demon-Haunted World: Science as a Candle in the Dark* and the quote goes on to say "When we recognize our place in an immensity of light-years and in the passage of ages, when we grasp the intricacy, beauty, and subtlety of life, then that soaring feeling, that sense of elation and humility combined, is surely spiritual. The notion that science and spirituality are somehow mutually exclusive does a disservice to both."

19- Peter Strople is one of the top Strategic Advisors focusing on Instant Change or what he calls "Focusing on NOW! He utilizes some of the world's top business, political and thought leaders to help assess strategic and tactical execution plans Instantly! Once validated he can create a base of investment and potentially revenue to continue to sustain the organization's initiatives.

Peter Strople is the 2009 recipient of the *IDA Founders Honors Award.* Peter was chosen based upon his passionate bridging of relationships and building of networks to help organizations serving the disabled, chronically ill and disadvantaged achieve new heights in care, reach and sustainability.

20- Herbert Jeffrey Hancock (born April 12, 1940) is an American jazz pianist, keyboardist, bandleader, composer, and occasional actor. Hancock started his career with trumpeter Donald Byrd's group. He shortly thereafter joined the Miles Davis Quintet, where he helped to redefine the role of a jazz rhythm section and was one of the primary architects of the post-bop sound. In the 1970s, Hancock experimented with jazz fusion, funk, and electro styles, utilizing a wide array of synthesizers and electronics. It was during this period that he released perhaps his best-known and most influential album, *Head Hunters.*

Made in the USA
Monee, IL
29 October 2022